Studies in the Quality of Life

Studies in the Quality of Life

Delphi and Decision-Making

Norman C. Dalkey

with

Daniel L. Rourke
Ralph Lewis
David Snyder

Lexington Books
D.C. Heath and Company
Lexington, Massachusetts
Toronto   London

Printed in the United States of America

International Standard Book Number: 0-669-81497-0

Library of Congress Catalog Card Number: 76-178916

Contents

List of Figures   vii

List of Tables   xi

Preface   xiii

Chapter 1   **Introduction,** *Norman C. Dalkey*   1

The Uncertainty of Important Issues   3
Group Judgment   4
Numerical Judgments   6
Points of View   7
Quality of Life   9

Chapter 2   **The Delphi Method: An Experimental Study of Group Opinion,** *Norman C. Dalkey*   13

The Spectrum of Decision Inputs   13
Two Heads are Better Than One   15
Delphi   20
Experiments   21
Comparison of Face-to-Face and
     Anonymous Interaction   23
The Nature of Estimation   25
Improvement with Iteration   29
Mechanism of Improvement   31
Supplementary Analyses   37
Feed-In of Factual Information   48

Chapter 3   **Experimental Assessment of Delphi Procedures with Group Value Judgments,** *Norman C. Dalkey and Daniel L. Rourke*   55

Introduction   55
Method   58
Results   68
Discussion   80

Chapter 4   **Measurement and Analysis of the Quality
                 of Life**, *Norman C. Dalkey,
                 Ralph Lewis and David Snyder*   85

                 Introduction   85
                 A Preliminary Model for the Analysis
                    of Quality of Life   92
                 A Delphi Investigation of the Quality
                    of Life Models   96
                 Preliminary Application in Two
                    Individual Decision-Making
                    Contexts   109
                 Research Approaches   129

                 Notes   139

Appendixes   145

A   **Memorandum**   147

B   **Instruction Sheets for Alternative
                 Environments (Job Opportunities)
                 and Alternative Modes of Transpor-
                 tation Questionnaires**   151

                 Index   159

                 About the Authors   163

                 Selected Rand Books   165

List of Figures

2-1   Spectrum of Inputs   14

2-2   Worst Case: Median Better Than Half   16

2-3   Normal Case   17

2-4   Effect of Group Size   18

2-5   Reliability vs. Group Size   19

2-6   Distribution of Initial Answers   25

2-7   Distribution of Second Round Answers   26

2-8   Invariance of E/σ 27

2-9   Distributions of Individual Error
    Scores   28

2-10   Distribution of Scores, Reshuffled
    Answers   29

2-11   Cumulative Distribution of Group Error   30

2-12   Effect of Distance from Median on
    Change of Estimates   31

2-13   Improvement on Iteration   32

2-14   Mean Change of Estimate after Feedback   34

2-15   Change after Feedback   34

2-16   Bias, Round Two   35

2-17   Change of Group Estimate As a
    Function of Group Error   36

2-18   Individual Learning   39

2-19	Group Learning	40
2-20	Proportion Changing: Men vs. Women	43
2-21	Relationship of Accuracy and Changeability	44
2-22	Effect of Time to Respond	46
2-23	Group Self-Rating	47
2-24	Effect of Sequential Additional Facts	50
2-25	Accuracy Change in Single Questions with Number of Facts	51
2-26	Information Pattern for Differential Information Experiment	52
2-27	Summary of Differential Information Experiments	53
3-1	Computer-Generated Display of Factors from Analysis of QOL Similarity Ratings	63
3-2	Computer-Generated Display of Factors from Analysis of EE Similarity Ratings	64
3-3	Cross-Plot of Split-100 and Magnitude-Estimation Median Ratings for QOL Factors	65
3-4	Cross-Plot of Split-100 and Seven-Point Scale Median Ratings for EE Factors	66
3-5	Average Frequency Distributions	76
3-6	Most Deviant Distributions for Single Factors	77
3-7	Representative Distributions for Single Factors	78

4-1	Exponential Decrease of Positive Force	90
4-2	Relative Decline of Positive and Negative Force	91
4-3	Fluctuating Pattern of Q Over Time	93
4-4	Interaction of Determiners and Events	95
4-5	Characteristics: Interrelatedness	103
4-6	Aggregate Group Characteristic Ratings for Each Job-Life Environment	115
4-7	Theoretical Interaction between Values and QOL Characteristics	117
4-8	Aggregate Group Characteristic Ratings for Each Transportation Mode	122

List of Tables

2-1	Comparison of Accuracy of Group Medians	24
2-2	Improvement with Iteration and Feedback	30
2-3	Most Accurate Subgroup	32
2-4	Comparison of Distributional vs. Point Estimates	38
2-5	Changes in Group Response With and Without Feedback of Reasons	41
2-6	Improvement on Iteration With and Without Related Questions	42
2-7	Performance by Major and Sex	43
2-8	Effect of Iteration	45
2-9	Group Error As a Function of Standard Deviation and Group Self-Rating	47
2-10	Sample Question and List of Additional Facts	49
2-11	Average E/σ for Different Amounts of Factual Feed-In	52
3-1	Characteristics of Quality of Life	60
3-2	Characteristics of Effectiveness of Higher Education	61
3-3	QOL Factors	65
3-4	Educational Factors	66
3-5	Structure of Student Judgments	67
3-6	Summary of Results for QOL Groups	69

3-7	Summary of Results for EE Groups	70
3-8	Rated QOL Factors	71
3-9	Rated EE Factors	72
3-10	Differences between Round 1 and Round 2 Mean Standard Deviations for All Groups	75
3-11	Combined Mean Relevance Ratings: QOL and EE Groups	79
3-12	Reweighted EE Factors	80
4-1	Aggregated Interdependency Ratings	101
4-2	Aggregated Characteristic Weights	104
4-3	Group Ranking of Environments	112
4-4	Individual Rankings of Environments	113
4-5	Overall Rankings of Transportation Modes	119
4-6	Indicated and Computed Preferences for Modes of Transportation	120
4-7	List of Qualities Used in Four Delphi Studies of Quality of Life	130
4-8	Approach Summary	137

Preface

The papers collected in this book were produced at different times and involve different degrees of interaction with data. Some are close to "think pieces"; others are descriptions of specific experiments. Taken together, they express a relatively coherent set of themes. It did not seem to be appropriate to edit them into full coherence because the field is new and rapidly changing.

They are published at the present time because there is a rapidly mounting interest in methods of measuring individual and social well-being on the part of both public agencies and research institutions. In addition, the approach to decision-making inherent in the studies is finding widespread applications in business and industry. It is hoped that the material contained here will be interesting and suggestive to both public and corporate policy makers.

The studies reported here are the product of a group effort conducted over several years at the RAND Corporation. In addition to the names that appear as authors, there are many who have contributed in a significant way. Olaf Helmer (now with the Institute for the Future) played a major role in developing the basic notions of the Delphi approach, and in designing some of the earlier experiments. Bernice Brown, Richard Rochberg and Thomas Brown gave invaluable help in suggesting and conducting analyses of the data. Samuel Cochran (now at East Texas State University) gave crucial advice on structuring the experiments and helping to conduct them. And much of the work would have been much harder without the help of the programmer for the project, Carol Johnson.

Many of the groups involved in the exercises were volunteers who contributed their time and good judgment. These include members of the Rand staff and members of the RAND-University of California, Irvine, Federal Mid-Career Training Program. In addition, thanks are due to Fred S. Pardee, who gave active counsel and advice on the research reported in chapter 4, to Stephen H. Dole and Yehezkel Dror who read and made many helpful suggestions on this chapter and to Fred Ikle for his valuable and constructive criticism of chapter 3.

The work has been supported by the Department of Transportation and Air Force Project Rand. The Advanced Research Projects Agency also supported the methodological development.

1

Introduction

Norman C. Dalkey

Throughout the world, and in practically all walks of life, there is an increasing ferment concerning goals and values. Industrial enterprises are acquiring social consciences, and are pondering to what extent concerns such as environmental protection or responsibility to consumers should intrude on older goals like profits and share of the market. At national levels, there is growing acceptance of the responsibility of public policy for the quality of life of citizens, and a growing demand for a system of social accounting to balance economic and national security objectives. For individuals, the weakening of traditional institutional frameworks—home, church, the puritan work ethic—has raised a host of questions concerning what constitutes the good life.

The process of rethinking values is not a unique phenomenon in history. It probably has been occurring on a low key more or less continuously; and occasionally it appears to accelerate, as in the Renaissance, the early industrial revolution, or the present postindustrial revolution. One major new element in the present ferment is the degree to which the issues are apparent to large populations. In the nations of the Western world, the information media have been bringing into the consciousness of a large proportion of the citizenry both the events that dramatize the changes, and the issues themselves.

Another major difference in the present situation is the relative affluence of the Western world, which allows the diversion of substantial resources into the decision-making process and into social programs. The increasing role of government in health, education, welfare, economic regulation, and science are some of the visible effects of this reallocation of resources. Along with increased available resources, there is a rapidly increasing monitoring and information gathering ability due to major developments in communications and information processing. The opportunity appears to exist for very large improvements in the general well-being of people. But rather than creating optimism, the opportunity seems to be accompanied by an anomalous sense of disorientation—even to the question whether the United States is a sick society. Public surveys over the past decade have shown a decreasing percentage of individuals who report that they are very happy. Cantril and Roll detect a small, but significant decline in personal self-ratings between 1964 and the present.[1]

Some of the concern is generated by visible social trends—mounting crime, war protests, racial conflict, shifting mores concerning sexual behavior, demands by women for greater equality with men. But more generally, the increasing fractionation of social pressures among special interest groups—environmentalists, youth, blacks, the aged, chicanos, women, as well as the more traditional labor, religious, business, and political groups (the list is long and multiplying rapidly)—has led to a defocussing of social values. Our pluralistic society appears to have started a fissioning process with essentially no limit. The question as to where within this yeasty process is there something relatively solid to which social policy can be anchored is disquieting.

Without some technique for coming to grips with the value problems erupting throughout the nation, additional capabilities for social action are likely to augment the sense of disorientation. In the past, difficult problems of value resolution were left to the individual judgment of political, judicial or business leaders, or to that tangle of individual judgments called the political process. For better or worse, it seems likely that this way of life is on the wane. The U.S. public is becoming better educated, more knowledgeable about domestic and world affairs, and therefore more directly concerned with decisions that affect its welfare. At the same time, the limitations of the traditional political process for dealing with basic value problems is becoming more apparent. Above all, the instability inherent in the fractionation of interest groups is demonstrating itself in many dramatic ways. It seems likely that the demand for new ways of dealing with value conflicts will accelerate.

For reasons that will be emphasized repeatedly in the following pages, it is probable that individual judgment will remain a crucial factor in the process of value clarification. The questions are: Can the effectiveness of judgment be improved, and above all, is there a way of ameliorating the divisiveness inherent in the fact that individuals differ so widely in their points of view about basic issues?

Much of this book is concerned with the exploration of one approach to this set of problems; namely, the development of techniques of systematic group judgment (or, as it has been nicknamed, *Delphi*). Delphi is only one of many possible approaches and no claim is made that it will be the most significant in the long run. It seems probable that in the long run, increased scientific understanding of human nature and social processes will be the most significant input for dealing with value problems. For the short run—that is the next decade or so—Delphi appears to be one of the more promising techniques available to decision makers faced with the necessity of identifying and measuring goals and objectives.

The approach will be outlined in the remainder of this chapter. Succeeding chapters will discuss a variety of experiments and studies which explore its capabilities and limitations. Throughout, we have taken the attitude of the technologist, rather than the pure scientist. We have been most concerned with identifying techniques that are feasible in decision-making contexts and which have perceptible advantages over earlier techniques. On the other hand, wherever possible, we have attempted to use the data to understand more fully the phenomena underlying judgmental processes.

The Uncertainty of Important Issues

One of the plain facts of life is that practically all important decisions, whether at the national level, or at the level of everyday life, involve issues which cannot be decided on the basis of hard data or well validated theories. A typical example out of many is the question of whether increased law enforcement is the "answer" to mounting crime rates, or whether solution to basic social problems such as elimination of ghettos is necessary. There are many volumes of sociological studies, commission reports, and testimony before congressional committees related to this issue. And yet this huge mass of material is insufficient to determine unambiguously where the emphasis should be placed in "dealing with" the crime problem. The illustration is not isolated. For any major national issue, whether to install antiballistic missiles, or to soften penalties for drug usage, the available information—however extensive—is insufficient to select the appropriate action with high confidence.

The situation is no different for corporate decisions, for local government, or for individuals. Whether to marry (or divorce) a given person, which career to enter, whether to turn on or drop out—these are among the significant choices for which there is no simple decision formula. Surrounding such decisions there is a cloud of uncertainty, attended by mysterious things called "intangibles," which usually make it impossible to arrive at a firm choice. This means that ultimately, the decision must rest on the judgment of some individual or group.

A fairly good test whether a given question is highly uncertain is to ask a group of the most knowledgeable people on that subject that can be found and examine the distribution of answers. If the members of the group report much the same answer, there is a good likelihood that the issue is not highly uncertain, and there is even a good likelihood that the group answer is correct. On the other hand, if the group reports a wide diversity of answers, then there is a high probability that the issue is uncertain.

This test is not quite sufficient to be a defining property for an uncertain question because, on the one hand, convention (including cultural bias) can lead to similar answers to some questions which in fact are poorly known; and on the other hand, there are some cases where one individual (whether in the group or not) does know the answer, but the others are either uninformed or "blind."[a]

---

[a]Historical examples of these two anomalies are often brought forward to "demonstrate" that common wisdom is untrustworthy. An often used example of both is the majority view during the middle ages that the world was flat. A small group of educated men knew better. However, this is not a good example, since there would not have been a serious problem of identifying the more knowledgeable group for that question.

However, these two cases are rare. There is a widespread feeling, difficult to overcome, that if a group gives a wide diversity of answers to a question, one of the individuals in the group is correct—i.e., knows the answer—and the others are mistaken. On the basis of a rather extensive series of experiments we have conducted with group judgment, this appears to be an illusion. In those cases where a group of knowledgeable individuals reports a wide diversity of opinion, it would seem that in the majority of cases no one knows the answer. In fact, the diversity of opinion is a relatively good measure of the degree of lack of knowledge concerning the question.

The first basic consideration in the Delphi approach, then, consists in recognition of the high degree of uncertainty that surrounds important questions—especially questions with value content—and relaxing the desire to find the so-called right answer. It then becomes meaningful to ask how the diversity of information that leads to disagreement within the group can be amalgamated to lead to the best available answer to the question. Actually, even this weaker aim is too strong at present. There are many features of the judgmental process which we understand too poorly to define *best*, much less specify practical rules for attaining it. At present we are limited to rules for finding *better* answers to uncertain questions.

Group Judgment

When faced with an issue where the best information obtainable is the judgment of knowledgeable individuals, and where the most knowledgeable group reports a wide diversity of answers, the old rule that two heads are better than one, or more practically, several heads are better than one, turns out to be well founded. This subject is discussed at length in chapter 2. There it is shown that in its elementary form, the n-heads rule is a simple truism. The group as a whole encompasses at least as much (and usually more) information than any single member.

This simple truism is the heart of the Delphi approach to uncertain questions. However, beyond the truism, there are several basic issues: how to select the most knowledgeable group, that is, how to define and identify experts; how to put the diverse opinions of a group together in the best way; how much and what kind of interaction to allow among the group as it formulates its opinion; how much additional material to furnish the group as "feed-in"; and how to formulate the question so as to allow the best individual judgments possible. On some of these matters the following chapters contain experimental data. Some widely held beliefs concerning judgment and the best use of experts do not appear to hold up in controlled experiments. The belief that sharing information by face-to-face communication improves the group judgment is not substantiated. In fact, the notion that each member of the group should be as knowledgeable as possible is not strongly supported by experiment. On the other hand, common beliefs such as a group will be more accurate if it exhibits high agreement than if it shows large disagreement turns out to be (at least statistically) correct.

There may be several aspects of this research which appear puzzling to the reader. If face-to-face discussion degrades the performance of the group, why was this not discovered long ago? The answer is not simple, since there are many intellectual tasks where face-to-face discussion does not degrade performance. These are typically tasks where the group can monitor its own progress—where it can tell when it is getting closer to the correct answer—such as solving a mathematical puzzle. These tasks are different from judgments relevant to decisions under uncertainty, where the correct answer cannot be identified. In the second place, although face-to-face discussion leads to degraded performance it does not do so inevitably; and in any case the degradation is not so great that the group is still not better than a single individual.

There is an extensive lore about the defects of group decision, especially by committee. Much of this lore is pertinent. Examples: "A committee does not think—only individuals think." "A committee is something which, if you ask it to design a horse, will compromise on a camel." The first example is, of course, a true statement. Given our present technology for using groups in intellectual tasks, there is no reasonable sense in which a group can be said to think—the procedures consist of ways of amalgamating the products of individual thinking. This statement may not be true for the indefinite future. Much more powerful ways of using groups can be envisaged—for example, on-line computer systems with members of the group interacting with other members, with rapidly accessible data, and with sophisticated computations—that will look a great deal more like "cooperative thinking." We are still some distance away from this capability.

The second example illustrates a large class of troubles with group interaction which are discussed more at length in Chapter 2. The excellence of group judgment depends on the way in which the individual judgments are put together. Horse-trading—that is, compromising on differences by a bargaining process—is not an effective way to use the knowledge of individual members.

On the other hand, the lore contains a number of misconceptions. One of the more serious is what could be called the *lowest common denominator fallacy*— the notion that a group dilutes the more competent members by including less capable ones. It is the case that on simple estimates—i.e., answers to single questions of fact—there will usually be a few individuals who outperform the group. Typically, this is about 10 percent. If it were possible to know beforehand who would produce the most accurate answers, then of course only their answers should be used. In most cases it is not possible to identify the one or two individuals who would outperform the group for the uncertain questions relevant to policy decisions. However, the fallacy is deeper, and consists in the notion that formulating a group response (e.g., taking the average of a group of estimates) is the same as accepting the answer of the average member of the group. In general the error of the average of a group of estimates is much smaller than the average error. This is not a paradox or a play on words. In fact, this rather blank statement contains a large part of the explanation of the superiority of the group over the individual.

One of the most significant results of the experimental studies is the fact that rough measures of the excellence of the group judgment can be derived from the individual estimates. Thus, it is shown in chapter 2 that the dispersion (degree of agreement) is a statistically valid measure of the accuracy of the group judgment. In addition, a score formulated by taking the average of individual self-ratings of their knowledge on a given question is also a valid measure of the accuracy of the group. In the past, when committees or commissions have formulated advice to decision makers, it has been possible to reject these on the grounds that they represent merely one group's opinion. Recent cases of such rejections by the administration have been widely publicized. It would appear that this arbitrary treatment of a group's opinion is no longer defensible. It was possible in the past because there was no way to measure how good the group judgment was. It now appears feasible to put a measure on the group—a figure-of-merit, so to speak.

The long-range effects of this discovery can be large. Thus, it is meaningful to ask a politician who makes a recommendation concerning the good of the country to put a number on it, indicating how solid it is. Our experiments have shown that such a number is not empty. If furnished by a panel of experts, the figure-of-merit is only statistically valid; but this is a good deal better than no measure at all.

The same general notions give some impetus to present trends toward participatory decision-making, and diffusion of responsibility, both within industrial enterprises and within governmental organizations. This is not the place to expand on these notions—nor to list all the caveats that have to be born in mind in applying them—but the general idea that present organizational structures do not tap a large part of the available and relevant knowledge in the organization appears highly plausible on the basis of our experiments.

Numerical Judgments

Humans have a unique ability to make numerical judgments concerning intangibles. This has been known for a long time to psychologists who have used "subjective magnitude estimation" as a routine research tool. The list of nebulous items that have been investigated by subjective estimation (as opposed to objective measurement) is richly varied—probabilities of single events, intensity of sensations, seriousness of different kinds of crimes, relative status of various occupations, and so on. In many cases, subjective estimates approach physical measurement in their precision and reliability. This is particularly true of psychophysical judgments—estimating the relative intensity of perceptions such as light, weight, loudness, and so on.

Perhaps what is new in the present approach to decision-making is the not very profound suggestion that the same ability to put numbers on intangibles be used as a method of probing what are considered more important questions in public and everyday life. Here, the difficulties are aggravated by the strong feelings people have about the subject, and the relative importance given to what, in other subject matters, might be considered minor differences. Nevertheless, as the studies in the following chapters show, individuals can make numerical judgments concerning the relative importance of basic life values, and these numbers are not capricious. It is equally clear that just because the judgments are made in numerical form does not mean that they are as firm or repeatable as numbers arrived at by physical measurements. But the use of quantitative judgments make a large difference in the usefulness of the data for analysis and application of group techniques.

In addition, despite the limitations of numerical estimation, it appears to be the case that much more information can be transmitted using such judgments than the more usual mode of speech in value areas. The natural languages are heavily endowed with quasi-numerical expressions—*very, much, little, some, hardly, quite, often, few,* and so on. It turns out that many of these can be associated in a reasonable fashion with relatively precise numbers. The studies of Cliff,[2] using Osgood's semantic differential technique, indicate that adverbs like *slightly, pretty* , and *very,* modify the intensity of adjectives in a surprisingly precise fashion, independently of the particular adjective to which they are attached.

The step from quasi-numerical to numerical estimates is not a great one as far as obtaining judgments from people is concerned. There is a natural reluctance on the part of many investigators to ask unsophisticated subjects to produce numerical judgments—especially when the quantities being estimated are of the sort usually referred to as "subjective"; but so far as we have been able to see from our experiments, there is no increase in uncertainty in making statements more precise, and the uncertainty that is there is much easier to identify and measure.

Points of View

One of the dramatic aspects of applying systematic group judgment to uncertain questions is the astonishing diversity in points of view that emerge. There is not only the divergence in judgments concerning a given question that has been discussed in the section on uncertainty, but an even more profound divergence in ways of looking at issues, or, so to speak in total perspectives on problems. This is true even when respondents have what appear to be highly similar backgrounds and highly similar interests.

This phenomenon is well-known in young, emerging disciplines and is easily apparent on skimming any technical journal in one of the less well-formulated sciences, for example, in the social disciplines. It is not uncommon to find each of the ten or so papers in a journal devoted to a different way of looking at what is presumably a common subject. This diversity of approaches is not particularly troublesome in a developing science, where each reader can glean what he can from each approach, and go on to generate his own approach. In the long run, the vast majority of these approaches are either winnowed out, or merged with others to produce an increasingly coherent central corpus of knowledge. Or at least that has been the experience of the more highly developed sciences up to now.

But the situation is quite different when the issue is to obtain group judgments on matters of immediate concern. Unless the group has a common point of view on which they are making their estimates, each individual, so to speak, is answering a different set of questions. It is a common belief that among the diversity of points of view, one is correct and the others mistaken, and the only correct way to proceed is to find the "right" one. This is similar to the attitude noted earlier concerning estimates on uncertain questions—that one of the answers is right and all the others wrong. Again, from the standpoint of group judgment technology, this attitude is misleading. The diversity of points of view apparently arises from incomplete experience and individual "cognitive styles" on part of the members of the group. It seems reasonable to suppose that each individual point of view has something to offer. The problem then, is to find a way of merging the diverse set of perspectives into one aggregated group point of view. Once this has been accomplished, it is then feasible to go ahead with obtaining group judgments on the elements of the group perspective.

Techniques for merging points of view are in a very elementary state at the present time. The problem is related to dimension reduction. Each respondent sees the issue in terms of a particular set of important factors or dimensions, and if a list of these is obtained, it is usually the case that a very long and poorly structured set of factors results. A typical case in point is the quality of life study detailed in chapter 3. Forty upper-class and graduate students were asked to write down 10 or fewer characteristics of individual life that they thought were the most important in determining the happiness or well-being of a person. The group generated a list of 250 items, where some of the items strongly resembled some of the others, but almost all had special features that set them apart. The problem, in this case, was to aggregate the long list into a shorter list that would retain the insights of each participant, and at the same time be meaningful to the entire group.

There are a number of dimension-reducing techniques available—multidimensional scaling, factor analysis, cluster analysis—none of which are precisely applicable to the point of view problem, but they give some preliminary handles. In the case of the components of the quality of life, we used a cluster analysis technique to reduce the list to a set of thirteen interrelated clusters. The members of the group did not appear to have any great difficulty in comprehending the composite list, at least as far as rating the relative importance of the aggregated components is concerned. But we had no good measure of the degree to which each subject was interpreting the list in the same way.

This subject is in its infancy. It appears fairly clear that a great deal of the disagreement encountered on basic issues in corporate and governmental decision-making, as well as on issues of personal life, is the result of the diversity of pictures of the world that each individual develops for himself. The creation of more powerful techniques for pooling these pictures into a more common picture is one of the most promising possibilities for resolving point-of-view related disagreement.

Quality of Life

The notion of quality of life that underlies the studies in this book is somewhat different from the one used by the news media, and by most public officials. The more usual meaning is related to the environment and to the external circumstances of an individual's life—pollution, quality of housing, aesthetic surroundings, traffic congestion, incidence of crime, and the like. These are important influences on an individual's satisfaction with life. And they have the additional feature that they appear to be more manageable by municipal, state, and national programs than attitudes or feelings. But they form only a limited aspect of the sum of satisfactions that make life worthwhile. An important question for policy is whether they constitute a major share of an individual's well-being, or whether they are dominated by factors such as sense of achievement, love and affection, perceived freedom, and so on. To answer this question, a somewhat deeper look has to be taken at quality of life as the individual experiences it.

The approach we have taken is based on some underlying hypotheses. First, the basic components of the quality of life are common to practically all individuals, and are only weakly dependent on ethnic or socioeconomic status. This is little more than the statement that people are people, and the aspects of experience that make a large difference in individual happiness are part of being human. This hypothesis is in agreement with Rokeach and others who contend that basic value dimensions are common among most people.[3] but is somewhat more radical in combination with a second hypothesis. The second hypothesis is that differences between individuals in relative emphasis on the basic dimensions of quality of life (relative priorities) are due in large part to the fact that tradeoffs among the components depend upon how much the individual is receiving of each. These variations in tradeoffs are also part of the underlying value structures common to most people. The wealthy man may rate material comforts lower than sense of achievement, whereas the poor man may reverse this rating. But on the present hypothesis, this is not a difference in basic values. The same poor man, if he manages to become wealthy, will switch priorities, not because of any fundamental change in his value system, but simply because the relative value of comfort declines as more is obtained. To use a popular cliché as a further example, if an individual is receiving a full complement of love and affection, he may be willing to risk some of that for added novelty.

The notion of variable tradeoffs is well known in economic studies; it has not been so carefully investigated for noneconomic values. It sounds a little foreign to quality of life, involving as it does the connotation of transfer of values and substitutability. Neither of these two elements are intended in the present usage. All that is intended is that two different individuals, with quite different patterns of rewards in terms of basic values, can experience about the same level of quality of life.

Associated with these two hypotheses is the assumption that many attitudes and beliefs which are labeled values are disguised rules for obtaining higher levels of quality of life. In the language of decision theory, these rules are strategies (or rules for selecting strategies) and not payoffs.

The exploratory studies described in chapter 4 are intended to examine these hypotheses. In the spirit of the previous sections, we have assumed that the underlying set of basic values is incompletely perceived by most (probably all) individuals, and that a group point of view and a group judgment concerning the relative importance of the components will be both more complete and more accurate than individual points of view. It is not expected that the group point of view will be exact, or infallible. A number of studies, conducted with different kinds of groups and with an additional one from a foreign country, show a great deal of stability both in the identified components and in judgments of their relative importance. To this extent they are compatible with the uniformity hypotheses. On the other hand, the amount of dispersion in the judgments of relative importance indicates that the judgments have a high degree of uncertainty, and must be taken with a healthy degree of caution.

Unfortunately, none of our studies was large enough to delve deeply into the measurement of tradeoff variation. The studies can be thought of as examining tradeoffs at some (average) circumstance of the respondents. Since most of the groups worked with were either students or professional people, it is perhaps not surprising that similarities in the tradeoffs should show up.

The same approach can be taken to the formulation of basic objectives for a business firm, or for a government agency. The point has long been made that business firms pursue a number of objectives beyond profit maximization. This hypothesis is confirmed if a group of corporate executives are asked to list the characteristics of a company that are deemed important in determining how well the company is doing. We have run this kind of exercise with several groups of executives (they are not reported in detail because the exercises were proprietary). In general, the lists identified by these groups contain items like growth, stability, employee welfare, public image, excellence of product, competitive position; and also in general, several of these will be considered more important than static profit margin (return on investment). The situation appears to be that some subset of these objectives are explicitly recognized by each executive, and the others may or may not be hazily recognized in his thinking about the company. The comments about point of view are directly relevant here. Each executive has his own specialized model of evaluation for the company. Each is incomplete. Our experience has been that when the more complete list is made explicit, it is not rejected by the group, but rather is recognized as being a more comprehensive, and by and large more valid set of objectives than the individual models which it aggregates.

2

The Delphi Method: An Experimental Study of Group Opinion

Norman C. Dalkey

The Spectrum of Decision Inputs

One of the thorniest problems facing the policy analyst is posed by the situation where, for a significant segment of his study, there is unsatisfactory information. The deficiency can be with respect to data—incomplete or faulty—or more seriously with respect to the model or theory—again either incomplete or insufficiently verified. This situation is probably the norm rather than a rare occurrence.

The usual way of handling this problem is by what could be called *deferred considerations*. That is, the analyst carries out his study using whatever good data and confirmed models he has and leaves the intangibles to the step called "interpretation of results."[a] In some cases the deferment is more drastic. The analyst presents his study, for what it is worth, to a decision maker, who is expected to conduct the interpretation and inclusion in the total picture.

In describing the interpretation-of-results step, interesting words are likely to appear. These include terms like *judgment, insight, experience*, and especially as applied to decision makers, *wisdom* or *broad understanding*. These terms contrast with the presumed precision, scientific care, and dependence on data that characterize operations research. Above all, there is a slightly mystical quality about the notions. They are never explained. Standards of excellence are lacking. And there is more than a hint that the capabilities involved somehow go beyond the more mundane procedures of analysis.

Taking a look at the kinds of information that can play a role in decision-making, there are roughly three types (see figure 2-1). On the one hand, there are assertions that are highly confirmed—assertions for which there is a great deal of evidence backing them up. This kind of information can be called *knowledge*. At the other end of the scale is material that has little or no evidential backing. Such material is usually called *speculation*. In between is a broad area of material for which there is some basis for belief but that is not sufficiently confirmed to warrant being called knowledge. There is not good name for this middling area. I call it *opinion*. The dividing lines between these three are very fuzzy, and the gross trichotomy smears over the large differences that exist within types. However, the three-way split has many advantages over the more common tendency to dismiss whatever is not knowledge as mere speculation.

---

[a]The not infrequent case where the analyst "makes do" with faulty data or shaky models has been sufficiently excoriated in the manuals of operations research methodology.

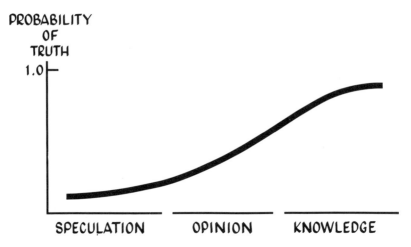

Figure 2-1. Spectrum of Inputs.

Where in this scale do the products of judgment, wisdom, insight, and similar intellectual processes, lie? Not in speculation, we hope. And, almost by definition, not in knowledge. The most reasonable interpretation would be that these are flattering names for kinds of opinion.[b]

Unfortunately, there is no practical, objective measure for the dimension of evidence sketched in figure 2-1. The best we have is an intuitive and rough feeling for the scale.[c] The prototype of knowledge may be found in the systematized, experimentally confirmed propositions of the natural sciences. But many of the assertions in the area that is called common sense have an equal solidity; for example, the gross features of gravity—unsupported objects fall to the surface of the earth, the permanence of objects, and the like. A large part of the empirical generalizations of common technology are equally well confirmed. The technologist's criterion—"Does it work?"—is at least as effective in eliminating unfounded notions as the scientist's "Is it confirmed by laboratory experiment?"

In the following it will be taken for granted that methods of dealing with material in the area of knowledge are in reasonably good order. There are, of course, many problems of detail—the warrantability of extrapolation, the application of statistical measures where underlying distributions are unknown, and the like. But these difficulties are small compared with the conceptual vacuum that appears to exist in the area of opinion.

---

[b]One might say, "Wisdom is opinion with charisma."
[c]A Delphi approach for locating assertions on the evidence scale is discussed on pp. 47-48.

With respect to speculation, it appears very difficult to say anything wise other than to avoid it whenever possible. That isn't very helpful. It appears likely that most major policy decisions involve more than a dash of speculative inputs. Some of the general results described below are applicable to speculation, but how useful it is to the decision maker to furnish him with refined speculation is hard to say.

This report sidesteps the even more difficult issue raised by the fact that most practical decision situations involve a mixture of all three types of information. The delicate balancing of the weight to give each kind of material is a second-level sort of wisdom that has not yet been investigated.

In discussions of policy analysis, it is usual to distinguish two kinds of assertions: factual statements and value judgments. It is an open question whether there is any basic conceptual difference between these two, but there are certainly very large practical differences. Group value judgments are discussed in chapters 3 and 4; the following sections are concerned with factual judgments.

With respect to factual statements, it is worth pointing out that the crude scale of solidity is related to the likelihood that assertions are true. In the area of knowledge, by definition the probability of an assertion being true is relatively high; for speculative material the probability is low; and for opinion it is middling (see figure 2-1). This point is rather vital. There is an irrepressible urge on the part of analysts to move the arena of decision entirely into the knowledge area. Sometimes this is possible. In general, it is not. When an opinion is expressed, it is an inescapable fact of life that whatever is said, there is a reasonable probability of its being false.

Two Heads are Better Than One

There is a kind of technology for dealing with opinion that has been applied throughout historical times and probably in more ancient times as well. The technology is based on the adage "Two heads are better than one," or more generally "n heads are better than one." Committees, councils, panels, commissions, juries, boards, the voting public, legislatures—the list is long, and illustrates the extent to which the device of pooling many minds has permeated society.[d]

The basis for the n-heads rule is not difficult to find. It is a tautology that, on any given question, there is at least as much relevant information in n heads as

---

[d]Most of these groups have more than one function. They can operate to transmit information, to coordinate action, to diffuse responsibility, to formulate policy, and so on. All of these functions are important. None of the discussion below should be taken to apply directly to these other functions. In the present context we are concerned with the use of groups to formulate judgments. If the results of the present study appear suggestive with regard to the other functions of groups, I can only hope that this tends to generate additional experimentation.

there is in any one of them. On the other hand, it is equally a tautology that there is at least as much misinformation in *n* heads as there is in one. And it is certainly not a tautology that there exists a technique of extracting the information in *n* heads and putting it together to form a more reliable opinion. With a given procedure, it may be the misinformation that is being aggregated into a less reliable opinion.

The *n*-heads rule, then, depends upon the procedures whereby the *n* heads are used. There is one kind of procedure and one kind of factual judgment where the *n*-heads rule comes very close to a tautology. Consider the case where the judgment required is a numerical estimate—for example, the date at which a certain technological development will occur, or the size of world population in 1990—and assume you have a group of indistinguishable experts with respect to this estimate; that is, you have no way of asserting that one expert is more knowledgeable than another. Is it better to select the opinion of one expert at random or to take some statistical aggregate of the opinions of the group? It is a near-tautology that you are at least as well off to take the mean or the median as to select an expert at random.[e] This is, of course, a very weak statement. It can be most simply illustrated by using the median as the statistical representative of the group answer. Referring to figure 2-2, it is clear that, independent of the distribution of answers, and independent of the location of the true answer *T*, the median of the individual answers *M* is at least as close to the true answer as

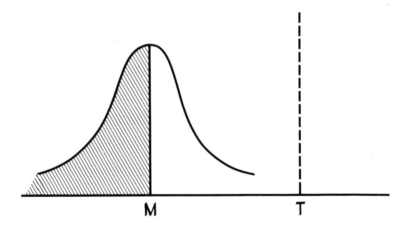

Figure 2-2. Worst Case: Median Better Than Half.

---

[e]The precise statement is: for the median, the probability that the median is at least as close to the true answer as any individual response is at least one half; for the mean, the error of the mean (measured by the distance to the true answer) is less than or equal to the average error of the individual answers. These two criteria are not equivalent, and for different decision situations one or the other could be more appropriate.

one-half of the group. If the range of group answers includes the true, then, in general, the median is closer to the true answer than more than half of the group, as in figure 2-3.

In practical situations, the range of answers is very likely to include the true answer, in which case the stronger assertion is valid. Figure 2-4 shows the dependence on group size of the mean accuracy of a group response for a large set of experimentally derived answers to factual questions. The curve was derived by computing the average error of groups of various sizes where the individual answers were drawn from the experimental distribution. The error is measured on a logarithmic scale.[f] It is clear from figure 2-4 that with this population of answers, the gains in increasing group size are quite large. It is interesting that the curve appears to be decreasing in a definite fashion, even with groups as large as twenty-nine. This was the largest group size we used in our experiments.

Another important consideration with respect to the n-heads rule has to do with reliability. The most uncomfortable aspect of opinion from the standpoint of the decision maker is that experts with apparently equivalent credentials (equal degrees of expertness) are likely to give quite different answers to the same question. One of the major advantages of using a group response is that this diversity is replaced by a single representative opinion.[g] However, this feature is

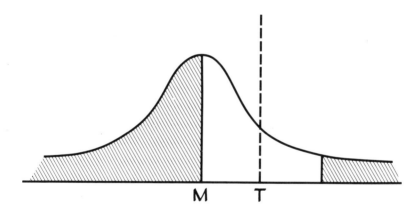

Figure 2-3. Normal Case.

---

[f]These were questions where the experimenters knew the answer but the subjects did not. The group error is the absolute value of the natural logarithm of the group median divided by the true answer. The groups used to construct figure 4 were "synthetic"; i.e., they were randomly selected sets of answers of the appropriate number drawn from the experimental distributions of answers.

[g]Whether this is the best use of group opinion, or whether the decision maker should take into account the full distribution of answers, and also make use of ranges of uncertainty on the part of individual respondents is an important topic in its own right, that will be partially explored later.

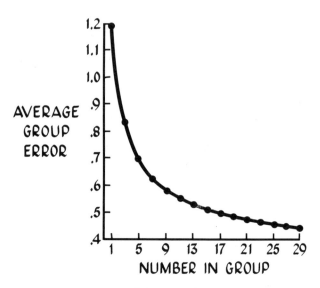

Figure 2–4. Effect of Group Size.

not particularly interesting if different groups of experts, each made up of equally competent members, come up with highly different answers to the same question.

In general, one would expect that in the area of opinion group responses would be more reliable than individual opinions, in the simple sense that two groups (of equally competent experts) would be more likely to evidence similar answers to a set of related questions than would two individuals. This similarity can be measured by the correlation between the answers of the two groups over a set of questions. But the assertion that groups will be more reliable than individuals is not a tautology. It depends on the distributions of answers that would be obtained from the total population of potential respondents, and it depends upon the method of selecting the subgroups out of this population. The result can be expected to hold if the distributions of answers for the potential population are not highly distorted, and if the subgroups are selected at random. There are clearly implications of this remark for the rules for selecting members of advisory bodies—in practice small advisory groups are probably never selected at random out of the total potential pool of experts.

For the analyst using expert opinion within a study, reliability can be considered to play somewhat the same role as reproducibility in experimental investigations. It is clearly desirable for a study that another analyst using the same approach (and different experts) arrive at similar results.

Figure 2-5 shows the relationship between reliability and group size for the experimental population of answers to questions already mentioned. It was

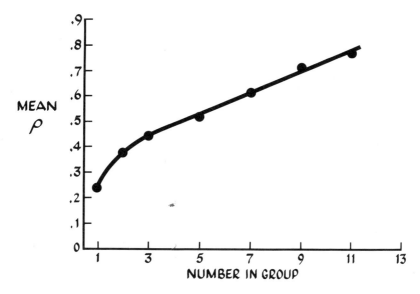

Figure 2-5. Reliability vs. Group Size.

constructed by selecting at random pairs of groups of respondents of various sizes and correlating the median responses of the pairs on twenty questions. The ordinate is the average of these correlations.

It is clear that there is a definite and monotonic increase in the reliability of the group responses with increasing group size. It is not clear why the relationship is approximately linear between $n = 3$ and $n = 11$.

In the area of opinion, then, the n-heads rule appears to be justified by considerations of both improved average accuracy, and reliability. The question remains whether these quasi-statistical properties of group opinion can be improved upon by allowing more direct pooling of information on the part of the group.

The traditional way of pooling individual opinions is by face-to-face discussion. Numerous studies by psychologists in the past two decades have demonstrated some serious difficulties with face-to-face interaction.[1] Among the most serious are:

1. Influence of dominant individuals. The group opinion is highly influenced, for example, by the person who talks the most. There is very little correlation between pressure of speech and knowledge.
2. Noise. By noise is not meant auditory level (although in some face-to-face situations this may be serious enough!) but semantic noise. Much of the communication in a discussion group has to do with individual and group

interests, not with problem solving. This kind of communication, although it may appear problem oriented, is often irrelevant or biasing.

3. Group pressure for conformity. The experiments of Asch demonstrate in dramatic fashion the distortions of individual judgment that can occur from group pressure.[2]

In experiments at RAND and elsewhere, it has turned out that, after face-to-face discussion, more often than not the group response is less accurate than a simple median of individual estimates without discussion.

Delphi

There has been a somewhat intermittent series of studies at The RAND Corporation since its early days concerned with the problem of using group information more effectively. The early studies were concerned mainly with improving the statistical treatment of individual opinions.[3] They indicated that some formal properties of individual estimates (precision, definiteness) could be used to rate the success of short-term predictions, and that background information (as measured by a standard achievement test) had a small but significant influence on the success of predictions. Both of these effects were fairly well washed out by combining estimates into group predictions.

In 1953, Dalkey and Helmer introduced an additional feature, namely iteration with controlled feedback.[4] The set of procedures that have evolved from this work has received the name *Delphi*—a somewhat misleading appellation, since there is little that is oracular about the methods.

The Delphi procedures received a very large boost in general interest with the publication of Gordon and Helmer's study of forecasting technological events.[5] In the area of long-range forecasting, it is difficult to dodge the fact that a large part of the activity is at least within the area of opinion, and possibly worse. That particular study happened to coincide with a surge of interest in long-range forecasting itself, with an attendant interest in the systematic use of expert opinion.

In the last several years there has been a very large increase in applications of the procedures, primarily by industry for the forecasting of technological developments,[6] but also by a variety of organizations for exploring policy decisions in areas such as education, public transportation, public health, etc. At present it is difficult to obtain a clear picture of how widespread the applications are; but a crude guess would put the number of studies recently completed, under way, or in the planning stages at several hundred.

In light of this widespread exploitation, the question of just how effective the procedures are has considerable practical import.

In general, the Delphi procedures have three features: (1) anonymity, (2) controlled feedback, and (3) statistical group response. Anonymity, effected by the use of questionnaires or other formal communication channels, such as on-line computer communication, is a way of reducing the effect of dominant individuals. Controlled feedback—conducting the exercise in a sequence of rounds between which a summary of the results of the previous round are communicated to the participants—is a device for reducing noise. Use of a statistical definition of the group response is a way of reducing group pressure for conformity; at the end of the exercise there may still be a significant spread in individual opinions. Probably more important, the statistical group response is a device to assure that the opinion of every member of the group is represented in the final response. Within these three basic features, it is, of course, possible to have many variations.

There are several properties of a Delphi exercise that should be pointed out. The procedure is, above all, a rapid and relatively efficient way to "cream the tops of the heads" of a group of knowledgeable people. In general, it involves much less effort for a participant to respond to a well-designed questionnaire than, for example, to participate in a conference or to write a paper. A Delphi exercise, properly managed, can be a highly motivating environment for respondents. The feedback, if the group of experts involved is mutually self-respecting, can be novel and interesting to all. The use of systematic procedures lends an air of objectivity to the outcomes that may or may not be spurious, but which is at least reassuring. And finally, anonymity and group response allow a sharing of responsibility that is refreshing and that releases the respondents from social inhibitions.

I believe all of these features of a Delphi exercise are desirable, especially if the exercise is conducted in the context of policy formulation where group acceptance is an important consideration. Like any technique for group interaction, the Delphi procedures are open to various misuses; much depends on the standards of the individual or group conducting the exercises.

Experiments

In addition to questioning the effects on free expression of opinion and group acceptance, it still must be asked whether the use of iteration and controlled feedback have anything to offer over the "mere" statistical aggregation of opinions. I put "mere" in quotation marks; In the area of opinion much can be gained by the simple arithmetical pooling of individual opinions as shown above. To get some measure of the value of the procedures, and also to obtain, as a basis for improving the procedures, some insight into the information processes that occur in a Delphi exercise, we undertook a rather extensive series of experiments at RAND starting in the spring of 1968. We used upper-class and graduate students, primarily from UCLA, as subjects. They were paid for their participation. For subject matter we chose questions of general information, of the sort contained in an almanac or statistical abstract. Typical questions were: "How many telephones were in use in Africa in 1965?" "How many suicides were reported in the U.S. in 1967?" "How many women marines were there at the end of World War II?" This type of material was selected for a variety of reasons: (1) we wanted questions where the subjects did not know the answer but had sufficient background information so they could make an informed estimate; (2) we wanted questions where there was a verifiable answer to check the performance of individuals and groups; and (3) we wanted questions with numerical answers so a reasonably wide range of performance could be scaled. As far as we can tell, the almanac type of question fits these criteria quite well. There is the question whether results obtained with this very restricted type of subject matter apply to other kinds of material. We can say that the general-information type of question used had many of the features ascribable to opinion: namely, the subjects did not know the answer, they did have other relevant information that enabled them to make estimates, and the route from other relevant information to an estimate was neither immediate nor direct.[h]

For about half of the experiments, the design called for a control group and an experimental group, each of about twenty subjects. For the others, the iterative structure allowed the group to be its own control. The experiments usually were conducted as closed information sessions, no inputs beyond the background information of the subjects being introduced. The standard task was answering twenty questions of an almanac sort. The questions were different from experiment to experiment (to preclude inadvertent transfer of information outside the experiments). The basic feedback between rounds was the median and the upper and lower quartiles of the previous-round answers. Additional feedback, summarized from subject responses, was introduced in some cases for experimental evaluation. Altogether, there have been some thirty experiments, involving close to fifty thousand answers to some two thousand questions on each of several rounds. I will not describe all the details of each experiment but will present a resume of the major results.[i]

The general outcome of the experiments can be summarized roughly as follows: (1) on the intial round, a wide spread of individual answers typically ensued; (2) with iteration and feedback, the distribution of individual responses progressively narrowed (convergence); and (3) more often than not, the group response (defined as the median of the final individual responses) became more accurate. This last result, of course, is the most significant. Convergence would be less than desirable if it involved movement away from the correct answer.

---

[h]An experiment comparing Delphi procedures with almanac type questions and with short-range predictions has been conducted.[7] The properties of the procedures that have been observed with almanac material were reproduced with short-range predictions.

[i]Details of procedure, the list of questions employed, and specific outcomes of the experiments are contained in the Rand reports listed in the notes.

Comparison of Face-to-Face and Anonymous Interaction

Two experiments were devoted to comparing the performance of groups using face-to-face discussion with groups employing anonymous, questionnaire-feedback interaction. The first experiment involved ten graduate student summer consultants to The RAND Corporation. These were divided into two groups of five, and the twenty questions were presented in four blocks of five each, following an ABBA design—A denoting face-to-face discussion and B denoting questionnaire feedback for one group, with the reverse for the other group. Thus, each group answered ten questions in discussion sessions and ten in questionnaire sessions. During questionnaire sessions, the subjects remained in separate cubicles. Approximately two and a half hours on successive afternoons were used to answer each block of five questions for each method of interaction.

The face-to-face groups were instructed to follow a specific procedure in dealing with each question. This procedure involved selection of a discussion leader at random, listing all information known to the group relevant to the question, devising several different ways of answering the question from the listed information, producing estimates by each of these ways, evaluating the relative solidity of each approach, and if possible, reaching a group consensus on the answer. For all but one of the twenty questions, a group consensus was arrived at.

The questionnaire procedure involved four rounds of estimates, feedback of medians and quartiles from the previous rounds, and reestimates. In addition, on some of the rounds the subjects were asked to rate their competence on the questions and to submit reasons for their answers. These additional features will be discussed in a later section.

The basic result was that the median response of the questionnaire group was more accurate in thirteen cases, and the consensus of the face-to-face group was more accurate in seven cases. Considered as an isolated experiment, this result is not statistically significant, a fact that is borne out by an analysis of variance.[j] However, when this experiment is considered along with several others showing the same kind of outcome, the results appear more significant.

The second experiment used a different design. We considered the possibility that five subjects were already a "large" group for face-to-face discussion. Accordingly, we took a group of twenty-three respondents, obtained their initial estimates on twenty questions individually, and then divided them into seven groups of three and one group of two. The medians and quartiles of the total group on the first round were fed back and each subject again made an individual estimate. The small groups then discussed the questions one at a time and again made individual estimates for each question. In the instructions for the discussion groups, some of the difficulties with face-to-face interaction that had

---

[j]An analysis of sums of ranks did reveal a statistically significant lower sum of ranks for the questionnaire group.

been identified in experiments at RAND and elsewhere were outlined, and the groups were requested to guard against the biasing influences whenever possible.

The basic outcome of this experiment is given in table 2-1.

The picture presented by these results is not as clear cut as that from the first experiment. The improvement (difference between more and less accurate) between rounds one and two is somewhat greater than the improvement between rounds one and three. From this point of view, the overall improvement would have been greater without the discussion.

The outcomes of these two experiments are in accord with the results obtained by Campbell.[8] In Campbell's study, a group of graduate students, some with business experience, first underwent an exercise designed to compare Delphi procedures with so-called normal procedures for making short-range forecasts of a set of sixteen economic indices. The normal procedures were not defined—whatever methods the subjects wished to use. Free communication was allowed the non-Delphi groups. The Delphi forecasts were, on the final (fourth) round, more accurate in thirteen cases; the normal procedures were more accurate in two cases. This result is highly favorable with respect to the comparison of systematic and controlled interaction as against informal interaction.

Of more direct relevance to the comparison of face-to-face and Delphi procedures was an exercise Campbell conducted at the end of the Delphi study. The teams were called together in face-to-face sessions and requested to discuss either four or five (depending on the time available) of the sixteen indices and come up with a consensus answer. For the two groups that had engaged in the Delphi exercises, the post-discussion led to a degradation of answers in three out of four and in four out of five cases. On the other hand, the unstructured interaction groups profited by the discussion in three out of four and in three out of five cases.

Although these three experiments do not yield a clear and simple outcome, the negative conclusion that discussion does not display an advantage over statistical aggregation appears well confirmed; and the overall weight of the experiments tends to confirm the hypothesis that, more often than not,

Table 2-1
Comparison of Accuracy of Group Medians after Controlled Feedback and after Discussion

	Change between Rounds 1 and 2 Delphi	Change between Rounds 2 and 3 Discussion	Change between Rounds 1 and 3
More Accurate	8	9	11
Same	8	3	0
Less Accurate	4	8	9

discussion leads to a degradation of group estimates. However, further experiments are desirable to establish the effect of face-to-face discussion more firmly.

The Nature of Estimation

One of our basic interests was to obtain a better understanding of the estimation process itself. The experiments were not designed specifically to explore this subject, but we hoped that the data would furnish some insights. As it turned out, the experimental data were very revealing.

The distribution of individual first-round answers for twelve of the experimental groups is displayed in Figure 2-6. In constructing this chart, the responses were normalized so that the mean and standard deviation of the logarithms of the responses of the group to each question were zero and one, respectively. The distribution begins at zero, since all questions asked (except for an inadvertent one concerning the lowest temperature ever recorded in Florida) have nonnegative answers. Drawn on the same chart is a log-normal curve with mean and standard deviation of one. The distribution of first-round answers is impressively log-normal.

The distribution warrants two comments. First, the range of answers is rather astonishing. Although not directly readable from the chart, answers to the same question often differ by a factor of 10^4. Second, the log-normality of the distribution indicates that the subjects were thinking as much in terms of ratios, or so to speak, in terms of the size of the answer, as they were about the precise magnitude of the answer. This suggested that a reasonable scaling of individual

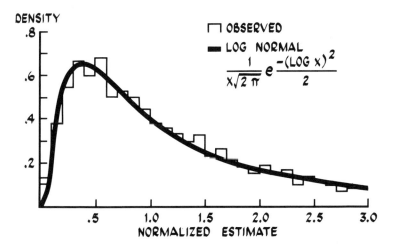

Figure 2-6. Distribution of Initial Answers.

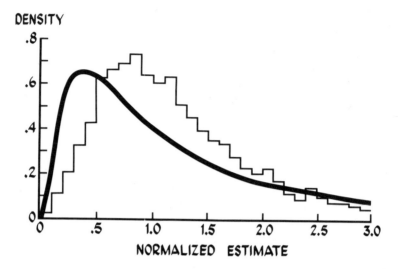

DENSITY

Figure 2–7. Distribution of Second Round Answers.

answers was a logarithmic transformation. This scaling has been used in most of the analyses of the data.

Figure 2-7 displays the distribution of second-round answers, where the first-round log-normal curve has been appended for comparison. The changes are manifest—there has been a large shift toward the mean. The shift toward the mean represents a convergence of answers toward the group response. However, the convergence is by no means complete; the second-round distribution still has a large range.

Additional analysis of the data shows that the log-normal is also a good approximation for the distribution of responses to individual questions.[9] Some data has been obtained concerning the estimated distributions on individual questions by individual respondents, but at present this data is insufficient to determine whether the distributions are also log-normal in the minds of the respondents.

Figure 2-6 suggests that there is a measure of order underlying the superficially chaotic set of answers obtained on individual questions. A salient issue in this regard concerns the relation of the accuracy of responses and the amount of agreement within the group. A widespread, but intuitive belief is that if a group displays a fair amount of agreement they are more likely to be correct than if they exhibit a wide spread of answers.

When a plot is made of the average error as a function of standard deviation, we obtain the set of points displayed in figure 2-8, approximated by the upper straight line (least squares fit). The small constant, 0.03, is probably within the noise level; and it appears reasonable to assume that the line passes through the

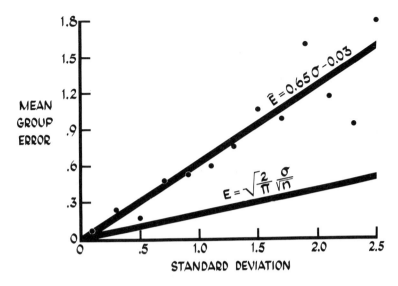

Figure 2–8. Invariance of E/σ.

origin. The lower line indicates the expected relation between average error and dispersion, assuming that estimation is a pure sampling process from a distribution centered on the true answer (for a sample of fourteen). The discrepancy between the observed and the expected error shows that the responses contain an appreciable amount of bias in addition to sampling error.

If we express the bias as the ratio E/σ, then the least-squares line in figure 2-8 indicates that the average bias is a constant. This result appears to be highly significant for interpreting the results of the experiments.[k] In the first place, it substantiates the intuitive belief that higher dispersions are associated with decreased accuracy. More to the point, the fact that the bias is a constant suggests that estimation (in the absence of complete information) is a relatively well-defined process. This conclusion is enhanced by the observation that the ratio E/σ remains relatively constant over a wide range of additional input information (see section 10, of this chapter, "Feed-in of Factual Information").

Figures 2-6 and 2-7 do not involve the accuracy of the responses. Figure 2-9 shows the distribution of individual scores where a subject's score is defined as the sum over twenty questions of the absolute values of the natural logarithms of his answers divided by the true answers. The distribution of second-round scores is also plotted in figure 2-9. The range of scores is again very large. For individuals at the far right of the curve, the average answer is off by a factor of about 8. At the low end of the curve, on the other hand, the subjects were off by an average factor of about 1.6.

---

[k]Finding an invariant of a process is always a refreshing, if somewhat rare, experience.

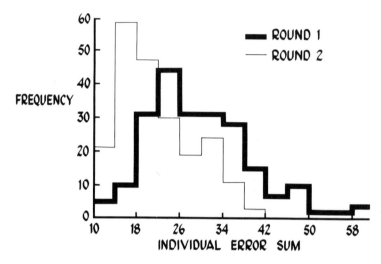

Figure 2-9. Distributions of Individual Error Scores.

It is natural to assume that such very large differences in scores on twenty questions indicate a wide range of ability to estimate. However, considering the large range of answers indicated by figure 2-6, a large spread in scores would be expected to occur by chance. A crude test of the hypothesis that more than chance is operating is simply to take the actual answers on each of the questions and, so to speak, deal them out at random to respondents and compare the distribution of scores so obtained with the observed distribution. This has been done in figure 2-10, where the computed "randomized" scores are displayed in the smooth curve. It is clear from the figure that the randomized distribution is a relatively good fit to the actual at the low end, but has a higher peak and a lower tail on the upper end. It would appear that more than chance is involved in the higher (lower accuracy) scores, and possibly also at the extreme low (high accuracy) end. We conclude that differences in ability to estimate the answer to general-information-type questions exist, but that these differences are heavily masked by chance.

Split-half reliabilities (correlation between accuracy on odd and even questions) for the first round range from about 0.4 to 0.6. This is not as good as would be desired for a measuring instrument. But the reliabilities do add to the presumption that differences in capability exist. A relatively extensive search for correlates of this presumed capability give a somewhat complex picture. This will be taken up in a later section.

The change from round one to round two shown in figure 2-9 indicates a large improvement in individual scores on iteration. Much of this change must be ascribed to convergence, i.e., to individuals whose first-round answers were

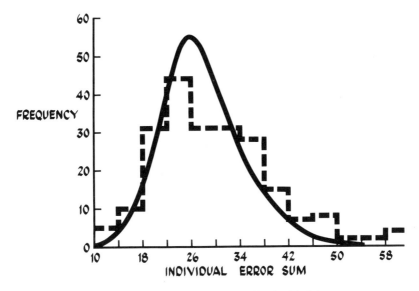

Figure 2-10. Distribution of Scores, Reshuffled Answers.

highly divergent from the group median and who improved by moving toward the median.

Improvement with Iteration

The data presented in the previous section mainly concern the estimates of individual respondents. When we turn to group responses (defined as the median, or for some analyses, the geometric mean of the individual responses), the picture is pretty much the same, but with significant differences in degree. Figure 2-11 presents a cumulative distribution of group responses on the first and second round for 287 questions. In this case, the abscissa is the error rather than the deviation from the mean. A cumulative distribution is used in this instance because the data are somewhat skimpy for a frequency distribution. Both curves are roughly log-normal. It can be seen by inspecting the two distributions that the second-round cumulative frequencies are uniformly above those for the first round. In short, on the second round, there is a higher proportion of second-round answers with lower errors; the second-round answers are to this extent better than the first-round answers.

The second observation with regard to the distributions is that the differences between them are small. The average improvement per question between round 1 and round 2 is 5 percent. The iteration step effected an improvement in accuracy, which was, however, less dramatic than the amount of convergence.

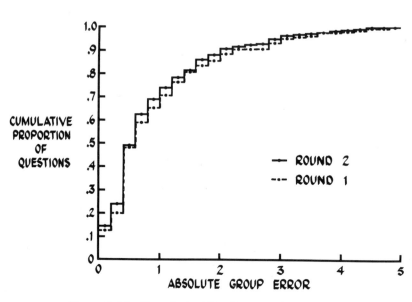

Figure 2-11. Cumulative Distribution of Group Error.

Table 2-2 presents the data on changes with regard to individual questions.

For about 64 percent of the changed estimates, the median improved in accuracy; for 36 percent, the median became less accurate. Perhaps more impressively, in none of the eleven individual groups represented in table 2-2 did the number of decreases in accuracy exceed the number of increases.[1]

This is, so to speak, the basic outcome of the series of experiments and furnishes the basis for presuming the Delphi procedures to be useful. However, as was evident from figure 2-11, the improvement between round one and round two is not particularly impressive. The question arises whether it is possible to improve on this result. To do so, it seems likely that a deeper understanding of the mechanism of improvement is necessary.

Table 2-2
Improvement with Iteration and Feedback

	Number of Questions
More Accurate	89
Same	80
Less Accurate	51

[1]For the grouped data in table 2-2, considered as a process with a single degree of freedom (under the hypothesis that a decrease in accuracy is as likely as an increase), $\chi^2 = 10.3$, $p < 0.01$. When the data are analysed in terms of the individual groups, using a trinomial distribution on better, same, and worse, and assuming that the likelihood of same is the proportion experimentally found, 4/11, the probability of outcomes as good or better than the experimental is 0.003.

Mechanism of Improvement

In order to have improvement, there must be changes of estimates between rounds. The most obvious influence producing change is the feedback of the round-one median. As figure 2-12 indicates, most of the tendency to change can be ascribed to one parameter, namely, the distance of the first-round answer from the first-round median. (The abscissa is in terms of distance from the median measured in units of the upper quartile minus the median for answers above the median, and in units of the median minus the lower quartile for answers below the median.) The likelihood of a change of estimate is very nearly a linear function of the distance from the median to about two quartiles, at which point it becomes erratic in a rather charmingly symmetrical fashion. Some of the erratic behavior beyond 2 can be ascribed to small samples; but some probably should be ascribed to the effect of feeding back the quartiles. The number of individuals who changed directly to the nearest quartile is much larger than would be expected from simple movement toward the median. In addition, we would expect that individuals who are close to the quartiles would be less likely to change than those who are far away from any reference point. There were not enough data to examine this hypothesis in detail.

Movement toward the median is not enough in itself to account for change in the median between round one and round two. In order for any change in the median to occur, it is necessary that some respondents make changes that cross the median. This can be clearly seen by assuming that all subjects simply move to the median. Although the degree of convergence would be as high as possible in this case, the median would not change. A fortiori, in order to effect a systematic improvement in the median, some process beyond simple convergence must be in operation.

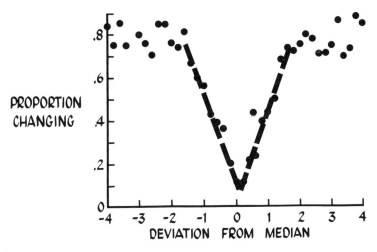

Figure 2-12. Effect of Distance from Median on Change of Estimates.

It is convenient to divide the group (for a given question) into the *holdouts*—those who do not change their estimates at all from round one to round two—and those who do change, the *swingers*. Figure 2-12 showed that the holdouts tend to cluster about the median. It is also the case that the holdouts tend to be more accurate in their first-round estimates than the swingers. Table 2-3 presents the comparison between the accuracy of the holdouts, swingers, and total group for round one and for round two. It is also evident from the table that the holdouts are more accurate than the total group on round one.

Figure 2-13 illustrates in schematic fashion the situation in round one and the effects of convergence. The mean of the group M_G will always lie between the mean of the swingers M_S and the mean of the holdouts M_H. Since the mean of the holdouts is closer to the true answer than either the mean of the swingers or the mean of the group, the true answer must lie somewhere in the shaded region. It is immediately clear from the figure that if the mean of the swingers moves in the direction of the mean of the group, the mean of the group will also move to the right and, in general, will improve. It will become less accurate only in case it moves across the mean of the holdouts, which requires that the mean of the swingers also move across the mean of the holdouts. If we define convergence as

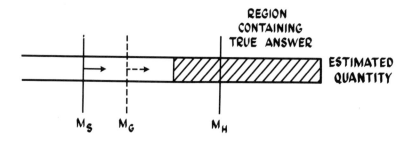

Figure 2–13. Improvement on Iteration.

Table 2-3
Most Accurate Subgroup (Geometric Means)[a]

	Round 1	Round 2
Holdouts	141	113
Swingers	73 ⎱ 94[b]	101 ⎱ 125[b]
Total Group	21 ⎰	24 ⎰
Ties	5	2

[a]This table is based on geometric means, rather than medians, to allow the differences to stand out more clearly. Although the geometric mean was slightly less accurate than the median, the geometric mean exhibited more changes between round one and round two.
[b]The total group is more accurate than the holdouts in the bracketed cases.

movement toward the mean on the part of these who move, then the kind of degradation mentioned cannot occur with convergence alone.

To sum up the preceding: A first approximation to a model of improvement on iteration is afforded by two assumptions. First, the holdouts are more accurate than the swingers and than the total group on round one. Second, on iteration the mean of the swingers moves toward the mean of the total group. These two assumptions are sufficient to assert that the mean of the total group will improve.

The first approximate model is insufficient to explain why the total group is more accurate than the holdouts on round two. The disparity is not sufficient to make much of in itself; however, the shift from 94 to 125 cases in which the total group is more accurate than the holdouts is inexplicable on the approximate model. In case the holdouts are more accurate than the total group and convergence is the only process occurring, then the holdouts will remain more accurate than the total group. The approximate model, then, is an explanation for part of the improvement in the mean of the total group on iteration; but a significant amount of improvement remains to be explained.

In Figure 2-14 the average amount of change is plotted as a function of two variables: the distance of the first-round answer from the median and the distance of the first-round answer from the true answer.[m] Distance is measured by the logarithm of the answer divided by the median in the first case and by the true answer in the second case; amount of change is measured by the average change in log scores in the appropriate box. We have already seen that distance from the median has a very strong influence (figure 2-12) with respect to the likelihood of change; figure 2-14 shows that the distance from the median has an equally strong effect on the amount of change.

It is clear from figure 2-14 that the effect of the median is much stronger than the effect of the true answer, almost to the extent that the median effect completely dominates the effect of the true answer within the region bounded by 3.5 on each axis. On the other hand, the effect of the distance from the true is evident. This is brought out more clearly in figure 2-15, where the amount of change is plotted against distance from the true for two constant deviations from the median. The curves (approximated by hand) indicate a definite increase in motion with distance from the true answer.

In a crude analogy with a physical model, we can speak of two forces operating on a subject to bring about a change of opinion. One force, which is a function of the distance of the subject's answer from the median, tends to change the opinion on the second round in the direction of the median. The other force, which is a function of the distance of the subject's answer from the

---

[m]In order to obtain sufficient cases for the entries, the two left quadrants have been reflected into the right quadrants, with quadrant II reflected into quadrant IV and quadrant III reflected into quadrant I. The assumption of symmetry was based on figure 2-12 and inspection of the full plot. The dashed entries indicate cases for which the number of instances were insufficient to give a reliable estimate.

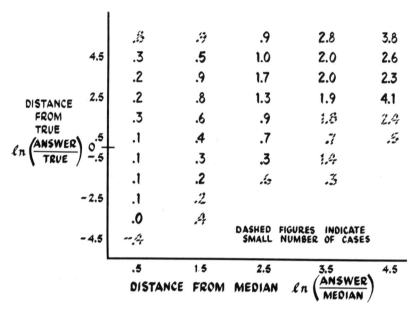

Figure 2-14. Mean Change of Estimate after Feedback.

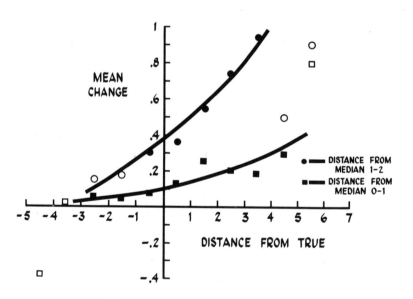

Figure 2-15. Change after Feedback.

true answer, tends to move the opinion toward the true. The "pull of the median" is much stronger than the pull of the true, but both operate.

In another way of speaking, it would appear that there is a certain amount of residual information remaining in the group after the first-round estimates have been expressed. In a fashion not yet explicable in terms of our data, the iteration and feedback step causes (or allows?) this additional information to be brought into play, with consequent improvement in the group estimate.

On the analogy with physical forces, the pull of the true answer is desirable. It has been thought in the past that the pull of the median is also desirable on the grounds that it leads to convergence and greater agreement among the respondents. In part this is due to the presumption discussed in the section, "The Nature of Estimation," that greater agreement implies greater accuracy. In part it is probably also influenced by several subsidiary issues—namely, it is easier to use an estimate with a narrow spread, and, if the concurrence of the group in some decision is required, greater acceptance of the decision would occur if opinions were fairly close.

The two practical problems—reduction of uncertainty and concurrence on decisions—need further study. But the presumption that greater agreement implies greater accuracy needs modification when the agreement results from convergence. Figure 2-16 shows the average error as a function of standard

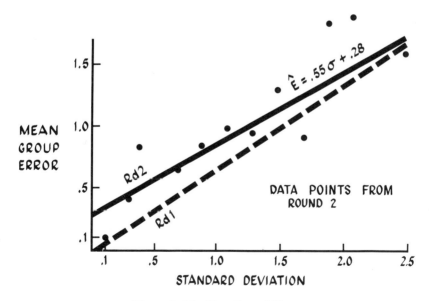

Figure 2-16. Bias, Round Two.

deviation for both round one and round two. The round two data are not as neatly linear as those for round one; but the important lesson from figure 2-16 is that the bias is greater on round two than on round one. There is good reason to assert that too much convergence has occurred; the increase in accuracy is not commensurate with the reduction in spread.

The question is: Can the pull of the true be amplified and the pull of the median be damped? There are some grounds for optimism. Figure 2-17 displays the amount of change of the group response as a function of group error. As might be expected, the amount of change increases monotonically with the amount of error. Also, as might be expected, the average change becomes negative (i.e., represents a net motion away from the true answer) as the initial group error becomes small; in effect, when the group is very accurate, any change is likely to be for the worse.

Figure 2-17 should be taken into account in assessing the significance of the earlier statement that the amount of improvement of the group response on iteration is small. For a large proportion of our questions, the initial error was small, and hence changes were small.

A somewhat more interesting question is whether this result, in combination with other results concerning the accuracy of group responses, can be exploited to improve the Delphi procedures. In general, it would appear that if the more accurate responses on round one could be identified, then with present procedures it might be better to omit the iteration step for those questions.

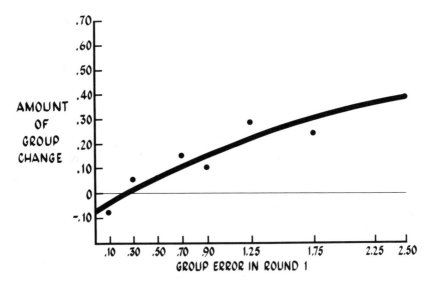

Figure 2-17. Change of Group Estimate As a Function of Group Error.

In general, the errors tend to be underestimates, i.e., the median response is smaller than the true answer in a large proportion of cases. This fact can be exploited by using as a group response a percentile larger than the 50th (median). Empirically, over the set of almanac and short-range prediction questions we have studied, using the 65th percentile as the group response leads to an average decrease of 20 percent in error. No experiments have been conducted as yet using the 65th percentile as feedback, but it seems likely that this would further decrease the error. Unfortunately, we have no data to determine whether this effect is dependent on the form of the question. All of our data involve the estimation of quantities such as dollars and populations. Whether the same effect is valid for estimation of probabilities or dates in the future, remains to be determined by further experiments.

Supplementary Analyses

In addition to the basic issues discussed above, the experiments generated data concerning a number of other pertinent features of group estimation. The items presented below represent a selection of the more interesting results from these substudies.

Distributional Estimates

A plausible hypothesis with respect to opinion is that estimators have in the back of their minds a rough probability distribution over the quantity in question; and when requested to produce a single (point) estimate, they select some measure of central tendency for this distribution. If this is the case, then theoretically, a more accurate estimate could be obtained by summing the individual distributions and selecting the mean or median of the composite distribution as the group response.

Two experiments were devoted to examining the effect of requesting distributional responses rather than point estimates. Subjects were asked to furnish the three quartiles for each question, that is, the number for which there is a 25 percent chance that the true answer is less, the number for which there is a 50 percent chance the true answer is less, and the number for which there is a 75 percent chance that the true answer is less. The three were called the low, mid, and high estimates, respectively. Somewhat to our surprise, the subjects had no difficulty making these presumably more complex estimates.

In the first experiment, there was a control group that made point estimates for the same questions. In the second experiment, there was no control group, and an evaluation can be made only by comparison with other groups in the series. In the first experiment, the experimental group was more accurate on both rounds, as shown in Table 2-4, the difference being heightened on round two. The second half of table 2-4 shows the improvement for the experimental and control groups between rounds. The experimental group demonstrated a greater improvement. Neither of these two results is statistically significant by themselves.

In the second experiment (thirty subjects), the median improved in ten cases, remained the same in nine, and became less accurate in only one case. Hence, the amount of improvement between rounds was much greater than for any other experiment in the series.

There is one consideration that clouds the results for the first experiment somewhat. Rather than feeding back medians and quartiles, the means of the three individual quartiles were fed back. It happens that for this particular group, the members tended to underestimate in most of their answers. As a result, the mean tended to be more accurate than the median. There is no way without further experiments to determine how greatly the improvement was dependent on this fact. In the second experiment, the median and quartiles of the mid estimates were fed back.

In a recent experiment, Thomas Brown has shown the feasibility of eliciting probability distributions for short-range forecasts, and assessing these with a probabilistic scoring system.[10] The outcome of this experiment does indicate that a group probability distribution formed by aggregating the individual distributions gives a higher expected score than a group probability distribution derived from point estimates.

Learning

A potential criticism of the procedures being investigated with regard to applications is that the subjects were fairly naive in the task assigned, whereas in

Table 2-4
Comparison of Distributional vs Point Estimates

	Round 1	Round 2
More Accurate	10	12
Same	2	0
Less Accurate	8	8
Improvement between Round 1 and Round 2		
	Experimental	Control
More Accurate	14	7
Same	1	12
Less Accurate	5	1

applications it would be expected that the respondents would be experts with long experience in making the kind of estimate involved in the exercise. The rather small amount of experimental data and much larger experience with nonexperimental applications suggests that this is probably not the case, but the evidence is certainly not sufficient to give an unequivocal reply.

One consideration here is whether the estimation task is a skill that can be learned. We devoted one experiment to testing the hypothesis that it was. In this experiment, the questions were presented one at a time. The estimation, feedback, and reestimation were completed before going on to the next question. In addition, after completion of the iteration, the group was told its second-round median and the true answer. Thus, members of the group could compare both their own performance and the performance of the group, question by question. The results are shown in figures 2-18 and 2-19. Figure 2-18 shows the individual performance as a function of question order averaged over blocks of five questions. There is a clear downward trend in round one, indicating some learning. This effect does not show up in round two, where the improvement between the two rounds is greatest for the first (least accurate) block.

Figure 2-19 is a similar curve for group scores, and no discernible trend is indicated. Furthermore, no group improvement between round one and round two is discernible for the later blocks of questions. We thus have no evidence for group learning with a sequence of twenty questions.

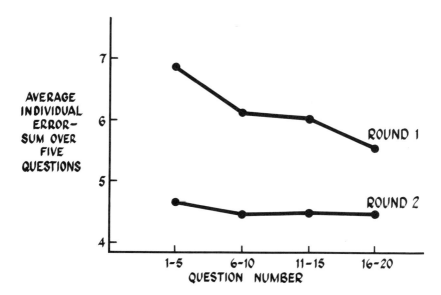

Figure 2-18. Individual Learning.

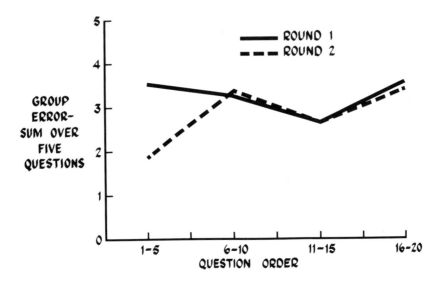

Figure 2-19. Group Learning.

These results indicate that, although a discernible learning effect exists for individual responses, this effect is dominated by the effects of feedback and aggregation into a group response.

Other Forms of Feedback

It has been customary in applications to include other types of feedback in addition to the statistics of the previous-round answers.[11] A typical procedure is to ask the subjects who are at the two extremes (i.e., in the top and bottom quartiles) on the first round to write down their reasons for their answers. These are edited by the exercise managers and fed back along with the second-round statistics on the third round. A fourth round may include the formulation of counterarguments.

In our first experiment comparing Delphi with face-to-face interaction, this procedure was followed in the Delphi sessions. There was no control group with respect to feedback of reasons. However, a highly suggestive outcome of this experiment was that the answers were most accurate on round two and became less accurate on subsequent rounds. Whether this deterioration can be ascribed to the feedback of reasons cannot be determined from the experiment; but we can conclude that there is no evidence that the reasons helped.

A second experiment was devoted directly to examining the effects of feeding back reasons, using a control group. The experimental group was instructed on the second round to formulate reasons for their opinion if their response on the second round was outside the interquartile range of the first round. These reasons were summarized and fed back on the third round in addition to the medians and quartiles of the second round. A control group underwent a similar set of three rounds, except that reasons were not asked for on round two but on round three. These were not fed back. The point of asking for reasons on round three for the control group was to determine whether the task of formulating reasons would have a discernible effect on the individual and group responses.

The outcome of this experiment is given in table 2-5.

Although none of the changes are significant in this experiment, we can say unequivocally that the addition of formulating and feeding back reasons did not increase the accuracy of initial estimates or produce greater improvement on iteration.

Two experiments were concerned with additional feedback of another sort. In this exercise the experimental group was asked to answer two related questions in addition to the primary question. Two hypotheses were being tested: (1) the task of responding to related questions would stimulate the subjects to consider a richer set of relevant factors, and thus improve accuracy; and (2) the responses of the group on the related questions, when fed back as medians and quartiles, would act as additional information available to the subjects and hence increase accuracy. The outcome of the experiment was indecisive. Table 2-6 indicates the comparison of improvement for the two treatments.

In the second experiment, there was no control group. Related questions were asked for ten of the twenty questions. In four of the ten cases with related questions, answers improved on iteration, in six cases they became worse. For the ten questions without related questions, there were five improvements, three worse, and two ties.

The two experiments give contrary indications with regard to the effectiveness of related questions. In the first experiment, related questions appear to improve the group performance both with respect to initial accuracy and with

Table 2-5
Changes in Group Response with and without Feedback of Reasons

	Without Feedback of Reasons			With Feedback of Reasons		
	Better	Same	Worse	Better	Same	Worse
Between rounds one and two	4	12	4	6	8	6
Between rounds two and three	4	15	1	4	8	8
Between rounds one and three	6	10	4	8	1	11

Table 2-6
Improvement on Iteration with and without Related Questions

	With Related Questions	Without Related Questions
Better	9	6
Same	6	11
Worse	5	3

	Accuracy Comparison by Question	
Experimental Group was	Round 1	Round 2
Better	10	12
Same	8	6
Worse	2	2

respect to improvement after feedback. In the second experiment (where the group was its own control), answering the related questions appears, if anything, to degrade the group performance. Probably somewhat more weight should be given to the first experiment, in which case the evidence is slightly in favor of including related questions. Additional experiments appear necessary before a firm conclusion can be reached.

Sexual Differences

The experiments verified two widely held clichés concerning the differences between men and women; namely, the female subjects were less accurate in their responses ("women don't have good heads for figures"), and they were more likely to change their answers. Figure 2-20 shows the comparison with respect to the likelihood of change for men and women. At any distance from the median, female subjects were more likely to change than male subjects.

Table 2-7 shows the relative performance with respect to accuracy of men and women. The entries are in terms of the percentile of the average score for the subgroup. Except for the anomalous case of female scientists (represented by only one individual), the percentile scores for the women are uniformly lower than those for the men.

One possibility is that the differences can be accounted for by some other factor than sex—the intelligence test scores, for instance.[n] In general, the distribution of CMT scores for women was displaced downward. The average CMT score for males was 105, whereas it was 88 for females.[o] When men and

[n]The Terman Concept Mastery Test (CMT), Form T, was administered to all subjects in four of the experiments.
[o]These are raw scores, not IQ scores.

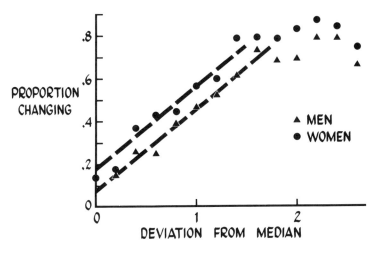

Figure 2-20. Proportion Changing: Men vs. Women.

Table 2-7
Performance by Major and Sex (Percentile Scores)

Major	Male	Female
Physical Sciences	44	71[a]
Biological Sciences	62	41
Psychology	50	36
Economics	62	42
Social Sciences	57	40
Humanities	75	26

[a]One case.

women are compared at the same CMT level, the differences in accuracy remain. However, the difference in changeability is much less noticeable at the higher levels of CMT scores. There doesn't appear to be a good explanation for this anomaly.

Another possibility is that accuracy and changeability are related—i.e., the females are both less accurate and less sure of themselves. This would suggest that there is in general a relation between accuracy and changeability for both men and women. Figure 2-21 shows the data analysed from this point of view. The hypothesis is borne out, but the women still show a greater amount of changeability than the men at a given level of accuracy.

We conclude that there is an identifiable difference between men and women on both accuracy and changeability. Whether this difference is "cultural" or more basic is, of course, open to conjecture.

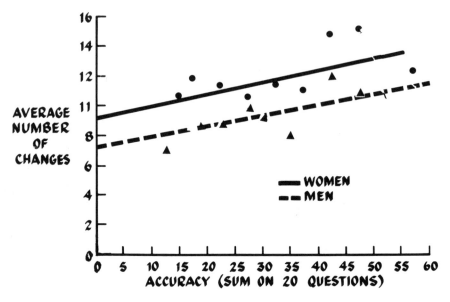

Figure 2-21. Relationship of Accuracy and Changeability.

Differences Due to Major

Table 2-7 also indicates the differences in percentile scores as a function of college major. The results were completely contrary to expectations. It had been expected that students whose major subject was one of the hard sciences would produce more accurate estimates than students from the humanities. In fact, the reverse is the case.

This result adds one more piece of evidence to the presumption that the realm of opinion is different from the realm of knowledge, and that methods which are appropriate for the latter may not be effective in the former.

Comparison with Simple Iteration

One obvious question is whether the improvement attendant on feedback is simply the result of iteration—rethinking. Two experiments were devoted to investigating this possibility. In the first, twenty-four hours intervened between round one and round two. In the second, a half hour intervened. The first experiment involved a control group that received feedback of first-round medians and quartiles on round two. The second experiment did not involve a control group. In each experiment, a third round with standard feedback was conducted.

The results are displayed in table 2-8.

Table 2-8
Effect of Iteration with and without Feedback

			Round 2 vs. Round 1	Round 3 vs. Round 2	Round 3 vs. Round 1
First Experiment	Without Feedback on Round 2	Better	9	6	9
		Same	2	8	2
		Worse	9	6	9
	With Feedback on Round 2	Better	8	5	10
		Same	7	11	4
		Worse	5	4	6
Second Experiment	Without Feedback on Round 2	Better	4	9	10
		Same	9	6	4
		Worse	7	5	6

The table shows clearly that without feedback there is either no improvement or a degradation. The same groups showed definite improvement with feedback.

Time

Three experimental sessions were devoted to examining the effect on accuracy of the amount of time allowed to answer. The time intervals used for these tests were 15, 30, 60, 120, and 240 seconds. The number of questions involved was 20, 30, 30, 30, and 10, for the respective time intervals. The results of these tests are plotted in figure 2-22. The point for 240 seconds is omitted because of the small number of questions involved. The plot shows a minimum for the average error in the vicinity of 30 seconds. Performance at the shortest time allowed, 15 seconds, is somewhat poorer than at one or two minutes.

The most significant feature of the results is the occurrence of a minimum. Fifteen seconds is barely enough time for the subjects to read a question and write down an answer; so there is no surprise that errors were high for this case. However, even the rather simple almanac-type questions we employed can involve a comparatively complex judgment. A question like "What was the popular vote for Kennedy in the 1960 presidential election in the state of Texas?" involves a number of factors: the population of Texas in 1960, the facts that Texas is a southern state, preponderantly Democratic, but conservative, and predominantly Protestant, that Kennedy was Catholic, and so on. Apparently, there is a fairly sharp limit on the number of factors and the amount of "processing" that can be dealt with profitably. At all events, we seem to have validated the advice frequently given in connection with objective examinations—"Trust your first estimate."

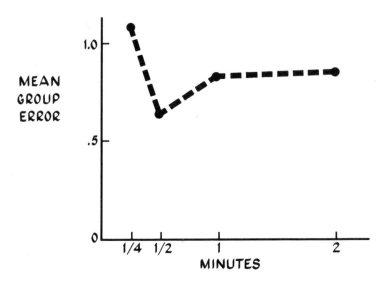

Figure 2-22. Effect of Time to Respond.

Self-Evaluation

In several of the experiments, subjects were asked to rate their answers in terms of either their confidence in their responses or their relative competence. Generally, a nominal scale of integers from 1 to 5 was used for these ratings. The group reliability for average self-confidence on individual questions was quite high. This was measured, for those cases where there was a control group, by correlating the average self-confidence of one group with the average self-confidence of the other over the set of twenty questions. Reliabilities ranged from 0.95 to 0.60 with a mean of 0.81. In short, the self-confidence ratings appear to be measuring something about the questions fairly well and not just individual differences in self-assurance.

Figure 2-23 shows the relationship between the group average of self-ratings and mean group error (curve approximated by hand). There is a clear inverse relationship between group self-rating and group error—in short, the higher the average confidence rating on a question, the smaller the group error. Hence, the average of individual self-ratings (the "group self-rating") appears to be a useful indicator of the accuracy of the group answer.

It was stated in the introduction that one of the major stumbling blocks in dealing with opinion was the lack of a suitable measure for the *solidity*—the degree of verification—of an assertion in the opinion area. It does not seem unreasonable a priori that group judgments of the degree of verification should be about as accurate and reliable as the group estimates themselves. Figure 2-23 bears out this presumption.

Table 2-9 shows the results of combining the dispersion-accuracy relationship and the group rating-accuracy relationship. Dispersion and group rating have a

Figure 2–23. Group Self-Rating.

Table 2–9
Group Error As a Function of Standard
Deviation and Group Self-Rating

Round 1 σ / Group Self-Rating	0–.49	.50–.99	1.00–1.49	1.5 up
1–1.99		1.386 / 1	1.114 / 11	1.706 / 26
2–2.49		787 / 4	.843 / 14	1.106 / 36
2.5–2.99	.655 / 1	.651 / 9	.767 / 9	1.083 / 22
3 up	.139 / 15	.339 / 14	.966 / 10	1.578 / 8

correlation of only 0.40; thus, there is the possibility that they can operate as separate discriminators with respect to accuracy. Table 2-9 indicates that this is indeed the case. For a fixed standard deviation, accuracy increases with increasing group rating, and for a fixed group rating, accuracy decreases with increasing standard deviation. The anomalies in the lower right hand boxes may be accounted for by thin statistics; the number of cases is indicated in the small interior boxes.

Table 2-9 shows that a combination of group self-rating and standard deviation furnishes a relatively sensitive measure of the average accuracy of the group response. The significance of this result can hardly be overemphasized. It opens the possibility that these two parameters can furnish a practical (albeit statistical) measure of the solidity of the outputs of a Delphi exercise.

Feed-in of Factual Information

In applied studies using Delphi procedures the group of experts interact not only with themselves, but also with a large body of external information. In addition, each expert has his own specialized background which is ordinarily too extensive to share with the other panelists. Two questions arise with respect to these circumstances: (1) To what extent does the lack of uniformity in background information within the group degrade its performance? (2) To what extent should additional external information be fed in to the group? The second question involves a subsidiary issue, namely, should the feed-in of additional information be uniform for all members of the group, or should there be a so-called division of labor in allocating new information for the sake of efficiency and as a recognition of the fact that the "meaningfulness" of the information will differ among the experts?

In actual practice, where the group is geographically dispersed and interaction is primarily by questionnaires sent through the mails, the amount of additional information that can be usefully transmitted is highly limited. It is assumed that the experts have already absorbed most of the relevant information.

It would require a large number of experiments to explore all of the issues involved in the two questions raised above. Two series of experiments designed to cast some light on these questions are now described.

The first set of experiments were concerned with the effect of feeding in various amounts of additional factual information. Four groups of upper-class and graduate students of 20, 20, 16, and 19 members respectively were used. The task consisted of answering a set of almanac questions, where each question was asked a number of times with an additional relevant fact presented on each iteration. A sample question with the sequence of additional facts is given in table 2-10. For two of the groups there were nine rounds per question, one without additional information, and then eight iterations with a new fact per

Table 2-10
Sample Question and List of Additional Facts

Question: How many telephones were in use in Africa in 1967?

Additional Fact:

1. The population of Africa in 1965 was 310 million.
2. There were 9.7 million telephones in use in the USSR in 1967.
3. There were 74 TV stations and 64 thousand TV sets in Africa in 1965.
4. The Gross National Product of the Union of South Africa in 1965 was 7.5 billion dollars.
5. There were 3.17 million high school students in Africa in 1964.
6. There were 12 million radio receivers in Africa in 1965.
7. The Gross National Product of Kenya was 270 million dollars in 1965.
8. There were 178 thousand telephones in Algeria in 1959.

round. For the other two groups there were seven rounds per question, six with additional facts.

The experiments were conducted using an on-line computer system. The questions were posed on TV monitors under computer control, and the responses were input directly to the computer using small individual consoles resembling the keyboards of desk calculators. The medians and quartiles of the answers on a given round could be computed immediately and fed back with the additional factual information on the following round. In addition it was possible to obtain judgments of the subjects' self-ratings of competence on each question, and ratings of the degree of relevance of each new fact. The four groups answered 11, 9, 13, 9 questions respectively. For most of the analyses below, only the 9 common questions are included.

As illustrated by table 2-10, in no case was the complete set of facts sufficient to determine the answer. The same set of questions was asked the four groups, and the same set of relevant facts fed in; but the order of presentation of the facts was varied randomly between the groups.

Figure 2-24 summarizes the data for all four groups with respect to accuracy as a function of facts fed-in. The dashed curve shows the same information for the total group of sixty-five respondents. This was feasible since the same set of questions was asked each group. However, the order of presentation of relevant facts was varied randomly among the groups. Hence for the combined group, the facts known to the different subgroups on a given round were not the same.

The very large effect of feeding in additional information is apparent. For the combined groups, the error is reduced by a factor of two after the introduction of four additional facts. The large differences between groups A and C compared with groups B and D appear to be related to a contextual factor; sessions with A and C were held in the morning, sessions with B and D in the afternoon. This may indicate either a motivational or fatigue effect.

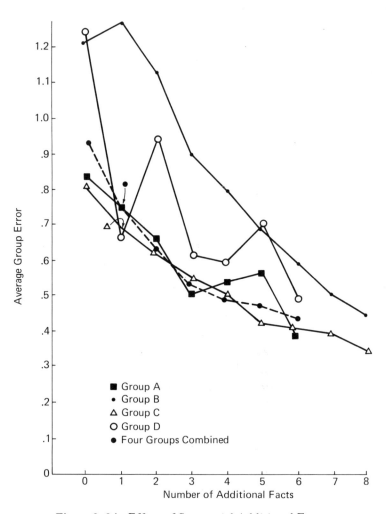

Figure 2-24. Effect of Sequential Additional Facts.

The only group for which each additional fact (on the average) produces a monotonic improvement is group C; for the other three groups, additional facts result in decreased accuracy on one or more rounds. Figure 2-25 shows two examples of changes from round to round on single questions. Negative error indicates the group was underestimating the answer, positive error that it was overestimating. For group A, question 1, the error changes sign with the addition of the fourth fact, and again with the addition of the sixth; however, the group decreases its absolute error at each change. Group B, question 3, on the other hand, gave its most accurate answer after the first fact.

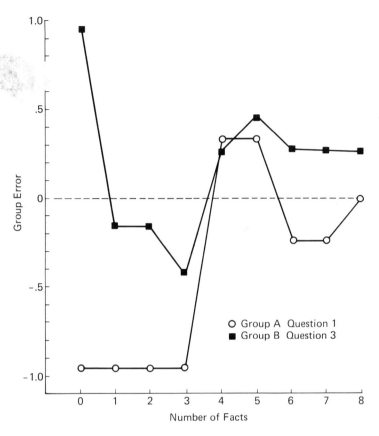

Figure 2–25. Accuracy Change on Single Questions with Number of Facts.

The combined curve in figure 2-24 indicates an overall decreasing return for each additional fact. The first fact produced a 20 percent reduction in error, the sixth about 9 percent. However, there is some additional improvement in accuracy out to as many as eight additional facts, and the curve appears to be still declining at that point.

A significant feature of the process of sequential feed-in of additional facts is that the standard deviation of the responses declines roughly in proportion to the decrease in error. Table 2-11 displays the average of the ratio E/σ for four points along the curve. There is a slight increase in the ratio (indicating a small reduction in bias) after the first fact, and then it remains at nearly the same level out to six or eight additional facts. This near constancy of the bias over a wide range of factual inputs is a further confirmation of the earlier conclusion that estimation is a well-defined process.

Table 2-11
Average E/σ for Different Amounts of Factual Feed-in

Round 1 (No additional facts)	.40
Round 2 (One additional fact)	.48
Round 5 (Four additional facts)	.50
Round 7 or 9 (Six or Eight additional facts)	.45

One suggestive feature of the data in figure 2-24 is the fact that by and large the combined group is superior to most of the individual groups, and at four facts is superior to all the individual groups. This could be due solely to a size-effect, but also, it could be due to the fact that the total group combines the disparate information among the subgroups.

In the second set of experiments, the subject of differential information within the group was dealt with explicitly. In this experiment two groups of twenty were formed. The task was to answer thirty almanac questions. One group—called the synthetic experts—were furnished four additional facts per question on the second round. The other group—called the synthetic laymen— was divided into four subgroups of five each, where each subgroup received only one of the relevant facts. Thus, for each question, each of the individuals in the synthetic expert group knew four relevant facts, whereas each individual in the synthetic laymen group knew only one fact. However the group of synthetic laymen as a whole knew all four facts. This structure is illustrated in figure 2-26.

There was no interaction within the groups between rounds. On round one the groups made their estimates with no additional information. On round two

Synthetic Laymen
(each receives one
fact)

Synthetic Experts
(each receives four
facts)

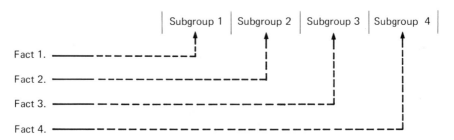

Figure 2-26. Information Pattern for Differential Information Experiment.

they answered the same questions, with either one or four additional facts. The results are summarized in figure 2-27, where the combined group accuracies from the sequential facts experiment are included for comparison (solid circles). The ordinate is relative error; the error with no facts is normalized to one.

The group receiving four facts (synthetic experts) in one package (slashed triangle) did slightly better than the group receiving four facts in sequence. The more interesting result is that the group receiving only one fact per individual (synthetic laymen) did nearly as well (slashed ellipse). The difference in accuracy between the two groups is not statistically significant.[P] On a replication of this experiment with new groups in which the synthetic laymen received two facts per respondent rather than one, their performance was not quite as good as the group with just one fact (slashed and open triangles). Again, however, the difference in accuracy of the synthetic laymen and the synthetic experts is not statistically significant. The fact that the small difference is in the same direction

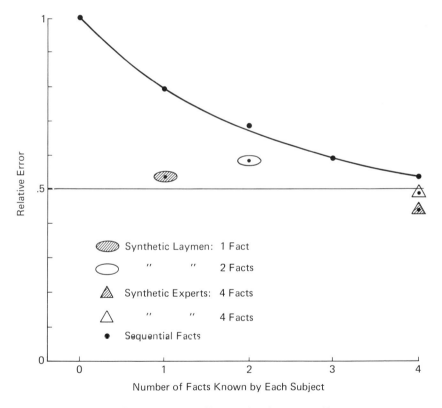

Figure 2-27. Summary of Differential Information Experiments.

[P]The F-ratio is 0.112 which for one degree of freedom gives $p \gg 0.05$.

for each of the experiments suggests that there is some advantage to giving all the information to each member of the group.

The upshot of these experiments would appear to be that additional hard factual information makes a large difference in the accuracy of the group judgments, but with decreasing returns (on the average) for additional information. On the other hand, differential information within the group does not degrade performance seriously, providing the group as a whole encompasses all the relevant information. Another way to put the same point is that the simple process of taking a group median appears to be a relatively effective way of pooling diverse information within the group.

The experiments thus give some information relevant to the questions posed earlier concerning group interaction. It has generally been thought that there is a large gain by letting the group share information. This may be a crucial procedure when the method of formulation of the group response is by agreed-upon consensus; however, if the group response is formulated by statistical aggregation of individual responses, sharing of information may be less important. Secondly, there may be a large gain in efficiency in a division of labor among respondents—apportioning the available external information among the group and letting the statistical aggregation of independent estimates perform the integration of this information.

3

Experimental Assessment of Delphi Procedures with Group Value Judgments

Norman C. Dalkey and
Daniel L. Rourke

Introduction

The last few years have seen a rapid increase in applications of group judgment techniques to public and corporate policy making. One of the more widely applied techniques is Delphi, already described in Chapter 2 and presented with a series of experiments designed to evaluate the procedures.

Most of the experiments which have been conducted to date have dealt with factual material. However, in some applications, the procedures have been employed to deal with a quite different sort of material, namely, value judgments. Typical is the use of Delphi procedures to identify and rate the objectives of industrial enterprises or to assess the relative importance of military missions. From the standpoint of the decision maker, opinions about values and objectives are just as relevant to decisions as factual opinions about consequences. Hence, the question whether Delphi procedures demonstrate advantages with value material of the same sort as those for factual material is a question of direct importance.

There are a number of difficulties in attempting to conduct experiments dealing with the excellence of value judgments. Above all, there is no generally agreed-upon way to measure the correctness of such judgments. Although there is some disagreement with respect to the proper measure for predictions of future events,[a] it is generally agreed that one relevant measure of excellence for factual opinions is just how close those opinions are to the true state of affairs. In general it is not difficult to arrange some scale whereby "closeness to the state of affairs" can be measured, although for opinions about the future, the investigator may have to bide his time until the future evolves. But in the case of value judgments, there is no generally agreed-upon corpus of facts against which the judgments can be compared.

Another difficulty with assessing the quality of value judgments has often been alleged: that they are emotionally loaded. Expression of such judgments is more directly tied to emotions than factual statements. Furthermore, commit-

---

[a]De Jouvenel refers to *futuribles* as something different from states of affairs past and present;[2] and some writers have been concerned about self-defeating or self-validating predictions.[3]

ment to those judgments is more central to the personality of the individual, so that the interaction of value judgments and other cognitive material is impeded.[1]

These difficulties might be considered enough to discourage any objective measurement of the excellence of such judgments. There is, of course, one type of objective study where this is no particular difficulty: that in which value judgments are considered simply as one aspect of human behavior, with no direct concern with what the judgments are about. Thus it is possible to study the genesis of judgments, the interrelationships between value systems, etc., without ever exploring the subject matter of these and especially without asking whether they are good or bad judgments.

However, this point of view is not the concern of the present inquiry. The usual point of view is that value judgments can be, in some sense, right or wrong. For example, when a corporate entity—for example, a board of directors of an industrial firm—asks what are the objectives of their organization, what are their priorities, which objectives are crucial and which only desirable, it appears fairly clear that they are not asking, "What are our capricious feelings about what we should do?" They would not be willing to accept the assertion that any other set of whimsical attitudes would be just as reasonable as the ones they express.

The same is true of the values people express with regard to everyday life, or the set of values that are ascribed to the nation. There may be violent disagreements on all of these, but there is little disagreement that the judgments themselves are usually not capricious.

It appears, then, to be the case in disagreements about values that most individuals would state that one side can be more correct and the other less correct without being able to specify how the value judgments can be validated. Exceptions are usually referred to as "matters of taste." As it turns out, it is not necessary to be able to specify what correctness or incorrectness means in order to say a great deal about better and worse judgments.

It was shown in chapter 2 that if a group of indistinguishable experts expresses a range of opinions concerning a given question, then the median opinion of the group is more likely to be correct than that of an (unspecified) member of the group.[b] In a like manner, if a group of equally competent individuals expresses a range of opinions concerning a value question, then the average opinion is more likely to approximate the correct answer than an individual judgment, given the presumption that there is a correct answer to the value question. In order to make this assertion logically acceptable, it is necessary to assume that the value judgment can be expressed in numerical terms. It appears that in most cases of practical import this can be done.

There are some other useful tautological consequences of the assumption that there is a correct answer to a value question. One is that the larger the group (maintaining indistinguishability), the more accurate the answer on the average. The other is that the larger the group, the greater the reliability of the answer,

---

[b]Strictly speaking, this should be read "at least as likely to be correct."

that is, the higher the probability that a similar group will express a similar answer.

All of these favorable aspects of group value judgments depend in part upon the degree to which it is considered that the group is judging something rather than simply reporting personal attitudes. Since we are precluded at the present time from a direct comparison of the group responses and an objective criterion, something weaker in the way of assessing the judgments is required. This something weaker is furnished by considering three of the necessary (but not sufficient) conditions for assuming there is a group judgment involved. These three conditions could be interpreted as a partial definition of the term group judgment for value questions.

1. *Reasonable distributions.* If the distribution of group responses on a given numerical value judgment is flat, indicating group indifference, or if it is U-shaped, indicating either that the question is being interpreted differently by two subgroups, or there is an actual difference of assessment by two subgroups, then it seems inappropriate to assert that the group considered as a unit has a judgment on that question.
2. *Group reliability.* Given two similar groups (e.g., two groups selected out of a larger group at random) the group judgments on a given value question should be similar. Over a set of such value judgments, the correlation for the two subgroups should be high.
3. *Change, and convergence on iteration with feedback.* This condition is proposed in part by analogy with results from experiments with factual material, that is, shifts of individual responses toward the group response and reduction in group variability. More generally, if members of the group do not utilize the information in reports of the group response on earlier rounds when generating responses on later rounds, it seems inappropriate to consider these responses as judgments.

In the experiments described below, these three criteria are applied to value judgments by university students concerning the objectives of a higher education and the objectives of everyday (individual) life. The students generated a list of objectives for these two areas, and rated them on a scale of relative importance. Three different rating methods were employed in order to test both group reliability and stability over scaling technique. Ratings were obtained on each of two rounds, where the results of the first round (the median and upper and lower quartiles of the responses) were fed back between rounds. The data generated by the value judgments satisfied the three criteria to about the same degree as corresponding data from similar groups making factual estimations. In short, the outcome of these experiments appears to be that the Delphi procedures—as far as we can evaluate them at present—are appropriate for generating and assessing value material.

The primary purpose of the experiments was to evaluate the Delphi procedures for value material, but the data generated concerning what the subjects considered important with respect to a higher education and to everyday life appears to have some interest in its own right. This aspect of the experiment will be discussed more fully later.

Method

In this study one group of subjects used the Delphi procedure to rate the relative importance of each of a set of factors in terms of the factor's contribution to a person's assessment of the quality of life. Our instructions to the subjects defined the phrase *quality of life* (QOL) to mean a person's sense of well-being, his satisfaction or dissatisfaction with life, or his happiness or unhappiness. A second group used the Delphi method to scale a set of changes in characteristics of students occurring as a result of their participation in the process of higher education. This scale measured the effects of education (EE) in terms of the importance of the changes for the student. These topics were selected because our subject population (UCLA upper-division and graduate students) could be expected to have informed opinions concerning each of them. The two groups received nearly the same instructions for the different topics and were for the most part treated identically.

The experiment required three sessions, the first two of which were devoted to the generation of the items to be scaled by the Delphi method in the third session. In the first session, each subject made up a list of from five to ten items important either for the assessment of the quality of life or for the evaluation of the effects of education on students.

The items from the QOL group (about 250 in all) were sorted into 48 categories of similar items, while the 300 items from the EE group were sorted into 45 categories. In the second session of the experiment the subjects who had made up the lists of items in response to the QOL questionnaire rated the similarity of all possible pairs of categories formed from the original QOL items. The EE group rated the similarity of all pairs of the EE categories. The similarity ratings were used to cluster the categories of the original items into super-categories. Thirteen supercategories or factors were formed from the QOL categories and fifteen from the EE categories. The relative importance of each factor was assessed during the third session of the study. The QOL group rated the importance of the QOL factors and the EE group rated the EE factors. A two-round Delphi procedure was employed where both groups revised their importance ratings during the second round in view of the median ratings for each factor obtained from the group's first-round ratings. As a check on the reliability of the ratings, the QOL and EE groups were each split into two subgroups and each subgroup used a different procedure to scale the factors.

The subjects were ninety UCLA upper-division and graduate students. They were recruited by advertisements in the school paper and were paid for their participation. No attempt was made to select subjects according to sex or field of interest.

During the first session, conducted at UCLA, subjects were instructed to list from five to ten items pertaining either to the quality of life or the effects of education. The subjects were randomly assigned to a particular topic so that forty-five subjects responded to each.

Subjects in the two groups were treated identically. The subjects were given printed instructions and a deck of ten blank cards. The instructions briefly introduced the subject to the purpose of the experiment and then requested him to list from five to ten items (one item per card) pertaining either to the QOL or the EE topic.

In the QOL condition, subjects were asked to list the characteristics or attributes of those events having the strongest influence on determining the QOL of an adult American. The subjects were instructed to ignore events concerned with basic biological maintenance, but not to overlook characteristics with negative connotations, for example, aggression. Subjects in the EE condition were asked to view higher education as a process which causes (or fails to cause) changes in characteristics of students. The subjects were requested to list those characteristics which should be considered in evaluating the process of higher education. Subjects were instructed to consider only undergraduate education while forming their lists.

Subjects were also instructed to rank their items from most important to least important. These ranks were used only as rough guides in the initial aggregation of items by the experimental team. Questions concerning the experiment were answered either by repeating or paraphrasing the instructions. No subject required more than half an hour to complete the first session. They were then given appointments for the second and third sessions which were conducted at The Rand Corporation in Santa Monica at intervals of one week.

Prior to the second session of the experiment, the items generated by the subjects in the first session were sorted into categories of similar items. Two sets of categories were formed, one for the QOL items and another for the EE items. The sorting was done by a panel of three; each member assisted in the design and execution of the experiment. Two criteria were used during the sorting of the items: (1) the perceived differences of any pair of items within a category were to be smaller than differences between any pair of items drawn from two different categories; and (2) no more than fifty categories were to be formed. Composite labels were developed for each category either by quoting or paraphrasing (or both) a few of the most frequently occurring items in each of the categories. The forty-eight QOL category composite labels are given in table 3-1 and the forty-five EE composite labels are shown in table 3-2.

During the second session, each subject was presented with a list of all

Table 3-1
Characteristics of Quality of Life

1. Fear, anxiety
2. Aggression, violence, hostility
3. Ambition
4. Competition, competitiveness
5. Opportunity, social mobility, luck
6. Dominance, superiority
7. Money, acquisitiveness, material greed
8. Comfort, economic well-being
9. Novelty, change, newness, variety, surprise
10. Honesty, sincerity, truthfulness
11. Tolerance, acceptance of others
12. Status, reputation, recognition, prestige
13. Flattery, positive feedback, reinforcement
14. Spontaneity, impulsive, uninhibited
15. Freedom
16. Communication, interpersonal understanding
17. Loneliness, impersonality
18. Dependence, impotence, helplessness
19. Power, control, independence
20. Good health
21. Failure, defeat, losing
22. Involvement, participation
23. Love, caring, affection
24. Self-respect, self-acceptance, self-satisfaction

25. Self-knowledge, self-awareness, growth
26. Self-confidence, egoism
27. Security
28. Challenge, stimulation
29. Privacy
30. Boredom
31. Escape, fantasy
32. Concern, altruism, consideration
33. Humor, amusing, witty
34. Relaxation, leisure
35. Sex, sexual satisfaction, sexual pleasure
36. Success
37. Achievement, accomplishment, job satisfaction
38. Faith, religious awareness
39. Peace of mind, emotional stability, lack of conflict
40. Suffering, pain
41. Stability, familiarity, sense of permanence
42. Individuality
43. Humiliation, belittlement
44. Being needed, feeling of being wanted
45. Conformity
46. Social acceptance, popularity
47. Friendship, companionship
48. Educational, intellectually stimulating

Table 3-2
Characteristics of Effectiveness of Higher Education

1. Self-awareness, increased self-understanding
2. Maturity
3. Ability to learn, learning to learn
4. Critical ability, questioning, development of a critical attitude
5. Honesty, personal integrity
6. Curiosity, desire to learn more
7. Social awareness, awareness of others
8. Social contacts, opportunity to meet a variety of people
9. Tolerance, decrease in prejudices
10. Open-mindedness
11. Understanding of others
12. Cultural awareness
13. Social issues, awareness of societal problems
14. Social skills, ability to get along with others
15. Broader outlook, new perspectives, scope
16. Political maturity, political awareness
17. Communication skills
18. Knowledge
19. Dehumanization, repressive bureaucracy
20. Career skills, job competence
21. Specialization, narrowing of interest to own field
22. Reasoning abilities, ability to think
23. Self-confidence, self-reliance, independence
24. Irrelevancy, prescribed education, educational trivia
25. Motivation, competitiveness
26. Isolation from real world, ivory tower syndrome
27. Impractical education, disillusionment with educational usefulness
28. Loss of creativity, loss of creative thinking
29. Greater creativity, expanding the imagination
30. Loss of idealism, general dissatisfaction
31. Responsibility
32. Sexual maturity, more liberal sexual attitude
33. Political disillusionment
34. New experiences, exposing to new activities
35. Narrowing of outlook, narrowing of values
36. Self-respect, self-acceptance, self-satisfaction
37. Dependency, prolonged youth
38. Synthesizing ability, a sense of organic relationship
39. Awareness of environment, relationship of individual with environment
40. Liberalization of social and political views
41. Purpose in life, development of life goals
42. Elitism, social status
43. Involvement, political involvement
44. Concern for society, fellowman
45. Relating to others

possible pairs of either the QOL or EE category labels. The task for all subjects was to rate the similarity of the labels in each pair. Every subject was given printed instructions, a list of the category labels, and a computer-generated list of pairs of labels. Each subject received a different random ordering of label pairs. The instructions informed the subjects that the items they had developed during the first session had been categorized to form the list of category labels. This list had in turn been used to form the computer printed list of label pairs. The subjects were instructed to rate the similarity of the labels in each pair on a 0-4 scale where the numerical ratings were tied to the following adjective scale:

4 Practically the same
3 Closely related
2 Moderately related
1 Slightly related
0 Unrelated

If a subject felt that the labels were connected, but in an inverse fashion, he was to use negative ratings, e.g., −4 being equivalent to "practically opposites." The following two examples were given: "Drowsy−Physically Tired," illustratively scored at 2; and "Drowsy−Alert," scored at −3. Both groups received the same instructions. The QOL group rated 1128 item pairs and the EE group rated 990. The experiment was conducted in two 1-1/4-hour periods with a 1/2-hour break between periods.

The means of the absolute values of the similarity ratings for each label pair were computed over subjects for both groups. These mean absolute ratings were then analyzed by Johnson's hierarchical clustering procedure.[4] In this procedure objects are clustered according to the similarities between them. The objects within a cluster are more similar to one another than to objects belonging to a different cluster. In addition, the procedure merges similar clusters into larger clusters in a stepwise fashion until all the objects are placed into a single cluster. Consequently, the user of this procedure must select the number of clusters which seems compatible with both the data and any theoretical or empirical predictions about the results of the procedure. The problem is not unlike selecting the number of factors to retain in a factor analysis. The use of the absolute values of the ratings "folds" the label pairs given the negative ratings into the same clusters. The clusters which were generated by this procedure are shown in figure 3-1 for the QOL groups and figure 3-2 for the EE group. Numbers across the top refer to the list of items in tables 3-1 and 3-2 respectively. The left-hand column indicates the similarity level at which the item is included in a cluster. The histogram of x's displays the progressive aggregation of items into clusters. For example, in figure 3-1 at the highest level of similarity (3.78) failure (21) and success (35) are associated−probably as straightforward opposites. At almost the same level, achievement (37) is joined

63

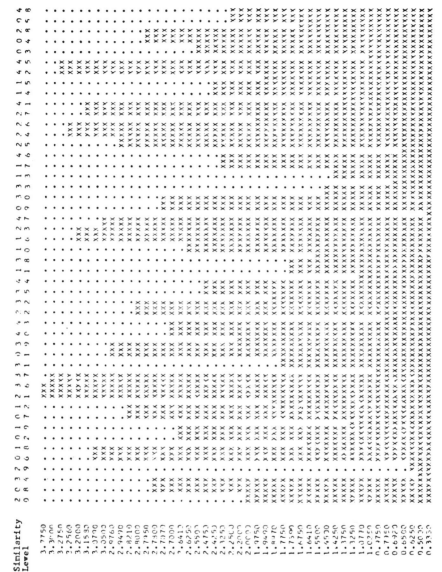

Figure 3–1. Computer-Generated Display of Factors from Analysis of QOL Similarity Ratings.

64

EE ITEMS

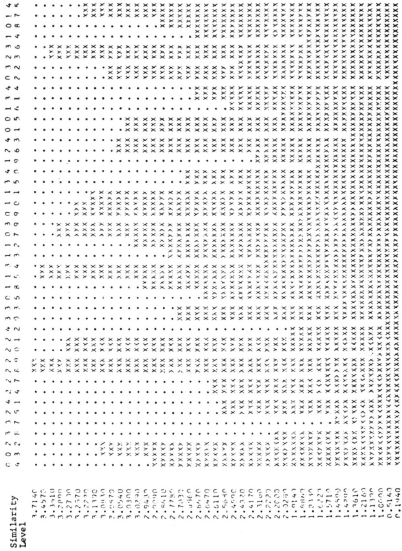

Figure 3–2. Computer-Generated Display of Factors from Analysis of EE Similarity Ratings.

MEANS OF ABSOLUTE VALUES OF SIMILARITY RATINGS

to the cluster. Nothing further is added to this cluster until level 1.9 when the previously associated pair, money (7) and status (12) are added. This is the "core" of characteristic 11 in table 3-3. The thirteen QOL and fifteen EE clusters which were selected are given in tables 3-3 and 3-4.

The task for the subjects in the third session of the experiment was to rate the clusters or factors in terms of their importance to the topic in question. The subjects who had developed the QOL factors rated them as did the subjects who generated the EE factors. The design of this session is shown schematically in table 3-5. As can be seen in table 3-5, the QOL and EE groups were each split into two subgroups, and each subgroup used a different scaling procedure. During the third part of the session, the QOL and EE group both rated the relevance of each of the EE factors in terms of its contribution to each of the QOL factors. Otherwise, the groups were treated identically.

In order to familiarize the subjects with the factors they would be rating, they were instructed to look over the factors and devise a convenient word or phrase label for each. The subjects were then asked to rate their self-confidence in working with each of the factors on a 1 to 5-point scale. The factors they felt most confident about were to receive a 5 and those they felt least confident

Table 3-3
QOL Factors

1. Novelty, change, newness, variety, surprise; boredom; humorous, amusing, witty.

2. Peace of mind, emotional stability, lack of conflict; fear, anxiety; suffering, pain; humiliation, belittlement; escape, fantasy.

3. Social acceptance, popularity; needed, feeling of being wanted; loneliness, impersonality; flattering, positive feedback, reinforcement.

4. Comfort, economic well-being; relaxation, leisure; good health.

5. Dominance, superiority; dependence, impotence, helplessness; aggression, violence, hostility; power, control, independence.

6. Challenge, stimulation; competition, competitiveness; ambition; opportunity, social mobility, luck; educational, intellectually stimulating.

7. Self-respect, self-acceptance, self-satisfaction; self-confidence, egoism; security; stability, familiarity, sense of permanence; self-knowledge, self-awareness, growth.

8. Privacy.

9. Involvement, participation; concern, altruism, consideration.

10. Love, caring, affection; communication, interpersonal understanding; friendship, companionship; honesty, sincerity, truthfulness; tolerance, acceptance of others; faith, religious awareness.

11. Achievement, accomplishment, job satisfaction; success; failure, defeat, losing; money, acquisitiveness, material greed; status, reputation, recognition, prestige.

12. Individuality; conformity; spontaneity, impulsive, uninhibited; freedom.

13. Sex, sexual satisfaction, sexual pleasure.

Table 3-4
Educational Factors

1. Greater creativity, expanding the imagination; loss of creativity, loss of creative thinking.

2. Broader outlook, new perspectives, scope, new experiences, exposing to new activities; knowledge; curiosity, desire to learn more.

3. Social awareness, awareness of others; awareness of environment, relationship of individual with environment; cultural awareness; social issues, awareness of societal problems.

4. Career skills, job competence; specialization, narrowing of interest to own field; elitism, social status.

5. Involvement, political involvement; isolation from real world, ivory-tower syndrome; dehumanization, repressive bureaucracy.

6. Self-awareness, increased self-understanding; honesty, personal integrity.

7. Loss of idealism, general dissatisfaction; political disillusionment.

8. Self-confidence, self-reliance, independence; self-respect, self-acceptance, self-satisfaction; maturity; sexual maturity, more liberal sexual attitude.

9. Tolerance, decrease in prejudices; open-mindedness; understanding of others; narrowing of outlook, narrowing of values; liberalization of social and political views.

10. Communication skill; relating to others; social contacts, opportunity to meet a variety of people; social skills, ability to get along with others.

11. Responsibility; concern for society, fellowman; political maturity, political awareness.

12. Motivation, competitiveness, purpose in life, development of life goals.

13. Dependency, prolonged youth.

14. Ability to learn, learning to learn; reasoning abilities, ability to think, critical ability, questioning, development of a critical attitude; synthesizing ability, a sense of organic relationship.

15. Impractical education, disillusionment with educational usefulness; irrelevancy, prescribed education, educational trivia.

about were to receive a 1. Next the subjects were requested to rate the relative importance of each factor in terms of the contribution of that factor to the general topic. Using the split-100 (S-100) procedure, QOL Group 1 and EE Group 1 were instructed to distribute 100 points among the factors so that the most important factors received the most points. Using the magnitude-estimation (M-E) procedure, QOL Group 2 was instructed to find the most important factor and give it a rating of 100. Then this group was asked to rate the other factors in terms of the most important one, so that a factor which they felt was half as important as the most important was to receive a rating of 50. The group using the rating scale (7-pt) procedure (EE Group 2) was asked to use a 1- to 7-point scale to rate the factors; a rating of 1 was to apply to "unimportant" factors, 4 to "moderately important" ones, and 7 to "extremely important" factors.

Table 3–5
Structure of Student Judgments for Session Three

QOL Group		EE Group	
Subgroup 1	Subgroup 2	Subgroup 3	Subgroup 4
Split 100	Magnitude Estimation	Split 100	7-pt rating scale
N = 20	N = 19	N = 19	N = 18

Part 1

Label factors	Label factors	Label factors	Label factors
Rate self = confidence with each factor on a 1–5 pt scale Split 100 pts among the factors according to importance of each factor	Rate self = confidence with each factor on a 1–5 pt scale Rate the most important factor with 100 pts and rate the other factors proportionately	Rate self = confidence with each factor on a 1–5 pt scale Split 100 pts among the factors according to importance of each factor	Rate self = confidence with each factor on a 1–5 pt scale Rate the importance of each factor on a 1 to 7 pt scale

Part 2

Revise ratings in light of group median and quartiles for each factor	Revise ratings in light of group median and ranges for each factor	Revise ratings in light of group median and quartiles for each factor	Revise ratings in light of group median and quartiles for each factor

Part 3

Rate the relevance of each EE factor to each of the QOL factors on a 0 to 3 point scale	Rate the relevance of each EE factor to each of the QOL factors on a 0 to 3 point scale	Rate the relevance of each EE factor to each of the QOL factors on a 0 to 3 point scale	Rate the relevance of each EE factor to each of the QOL factors on a 0 to 3 point scale

The subjects recorded their self-confidence ratings, factor labels, and importance ratings on preprinted response sheets. They also kept a record of their labels and importance ratings which they referred to during the second and third parts of the session.

During the second part of the session, the subjects again rated the importance of the factors with the same method which they used during the first part. This time, however, they were given information about the group's previous ratings on each of the factors. The QOL split-100, EE split-100, and EE 7-point rating scale groups were provided with the median and the first and third quartiles for each factor, while the QOL magnitude-estimation group was given ranges and medians which were normalized so that the largest median was 100. The instructions explained the meanings of the statistics and requested the subjects to consider this information in revising their estimates of the relative importance of each of the factors. The subjects were given twenty minutes to complete this part of the experiment.

During the third part of the session, the QOL and EE groups rated the relevance of each of the EE factors to each of the QOL factors. Each group received response sheets containing spaces along the top for each of the factor labels that they had developed during the first part of the session, and a list of QOL factors or EE factors, respectively, down the left margin. The subjects were briefly informed about the origin of the list of factors appearing on the left margin of their worksheets. Next, the subjects were instructed to familiarize themselves with these new lists of factors. Any questions concerning the list were answered by the experimenter. Finally, the subjects were required to rate the relevance of each of the EE factors to each of the QOL factors on a 0- to 3-point rating scale. *Relevance* was defined in the instructions as either "contributing to" or "means the same thing as." The 0- to 3-point scale was tied to the following adjectives:

3 Contributes strongly (or is pretty much the same)
2 Contributes moderately
1 Contributes slightly
0 Irrelevant

The subjects were allowed thirty minutes for the completion of this part of the session.

Results

Summary statistics computed from the QOL split-100 and QOL magnitude-estimation ratings on both rounds are given in table 3-6. Similar statistics for the EE group are shown in table 3-7. Both tables show the mean and median ratings and

Table 3-6
Summary of Results for QOL Groups

	Split 100, Round 1 N = 20			Split 100, Round 2 N = 20			Magnitude Estimation, Round 1 N = 19				Magnitude Estimation, Round 2 N = 19			
	Mean	Median	SD	Mean	Median	SD	Mean	G.Mean	Median	SD	Mean	G.Mean	Median	SD
1. Novelty	6.1	5.5	4.3	5.2	5.0	3.4	60	49	61	23	63	61	63	16
2. Peace of mind	9.2	10.0	3.6	9.3	10.0	3.1	94	94	91	16	96	96	94	10
3. Social acceptance	8.1	8.0	4.1	8.3	8.0	3.3	77	71	75	24	81	75	81	21
4. Comfort	6.4	6.5	2.9	6.1	6.0	2.3	72	69	63	22	73	71	71	19
5. Dominance	4.5	3.5	4.0	4.7	3.5	4.8	60	40	58	32	63	53	56	28
6. Challenge	8.3	8.0	4.8	8.0	8.0	3.3	72	65	80	25	80	76	82	18
7. Self-respect	11.1	10.5	4.4	11.9	11.5	4.1	98	98	100	15	99	99	100	13
8. Privacy	3.7	2.5	3.0	3.4	2.0	2.8	57	48	55	26	59	53	61	24
9. Involvement	6.7	6.5	3.4	6.0	6.0	2.6	72	69	72	22	73	71	74	18
10. Love	14.8	14.0	4.4	15.5	15.0	3.8	100	100	96	14	100	100	98	9
11. Achievement	7.6	7.5	4.6	7.5	7.0	4.2	79	78	79	16	79	78	78	15
12. Individuality	6.0	5.5	3.4	6.1	6.0	3.1	80	75	76	21	75	72	79	19
13. Sex	7.9	9.0	3.2	8.3	9.5	3.4	80	78	78	20	80	79	77	14

Table 3-7
Summary of Results for EE Groups

	Split 100, Round 1 N = 19			Split 100, Round 2 N = 19			7-point Rating Scale, Round 1 N = 18			7-point Rating Scale, Round 2 N = 18		
	Mean	Median	SD	Mean	Median	SD	Mean	Median	SD	Mean	Median	SD
1. Creativity	7.6	8.0	3.6	7.9	8.0	2.9	6.3	7.0	1.1	6.5	7.0	0.8
2. Broader outlook	11.3	10.0	5.0	11.4	10.0	3.5	6.6	7.0	0.7	6.7	7.0	0.5
3. Social awareness	8.1	7.0	4.5	8.3	8.0	3.8	6.1	6.5	1.1	6.3	6.5	0.9
4. Career skills	6.8	5.0	5.4	6.1	5.0	4.0	4.3	4.5	2.3	4.0	4.0	1.9
5. Involvement	3.9	5.0	2.2	4.8	5.0	2.7	3.9	3.5	1.7	3.4	3.0	1.5
6. Self-awareness	6.1	5.0	3.5	6.4	6.0	3.7	5.2	5.5	1.7	5.3	5.0	1.3
7. Loss of idealism	3.3	3.0	3.1	2.2	1.0	2.4	3.0	2.5	1.6	2.6	2.0	1.5
8. Self-confidence	6.3	6.0	3.2	6.6	6.0	2.2	5.4	5.0	1.5	5.3	5.0	1.1
9. Tolerance	6.6	5.0	4.3	6.8	6.0	3.6	4.9	5.5	1.7	5.2	5.5	1.3
10. Communication skill	6.7	6.0	3.7	6.8	7.0	3.2	4.8	6.0	2.0	4.9	6.0	1.7
11. Responsibility	4.6	5.0	2.0	4.8	5.0	2.1	5.1	5.0	1.8	4.9	5.0	1.6
12. Motivation	5.3	5.0	3.0	4.7	5.0	2.2	4.3	4.0	2.1	4.2	4.0	1.8
13. Dependence	2.2	1.0	2.6	1.2	0.0	1.7	2.7	1.5	2.2	2.1	1.0	1.5
14. Ability to learn	16.8	12.0	13.8	17.4	12.0	12.1	6.2	7.0	1.3	6.4	7.0	1.2
15. Impractical education	4.9	5.0	5.3	4.8	5.0	4.0	4.1	4.5	2.7	4.4	5.0	2.2

the standard deviations (SD) of the ratings for each factor. The factor identification numbers are keyed to the lists given in table 3-3 for the QOL factors and table 3-4 for the EE factors. In addition to the mean and median ratings, the geometric means (G-M) of the ratings are given for the QOL magnitude-estimation group. This was done in accordance with recommendations by Stevens concerning the proper method of averaging magnitude estimates.[5] Furthermore, the means, geometric means, and medians have been normalized so that the largest average rating is 100. These statistics are based on twenty cases for the QOL-100 group, nineteen cases for the QOL magnitude-estimation and EE split-100 groups, and eighteen cases for the EE 7-point rating scale group. The QOL factors are listed according to the decreasing split-100 second-round median ratings in table 3-8. The EE factors are similarly listed in table 3-9.

The agreement between the first- and second-round average ratings is very

Table 3-8
Rated QOL Factors

	Relative Importance
1. Love, caring, affection, communication, interpersonal understanding; friendship, companionship; honesty, sincerity, truthfulness; tolerance, acceptance of others; faith, religious awareness.	15.0
2. Self-respect, self-acceptance, self-satisfaction; self-confidence, egoism; security; stability, familiarity, sense of permanence; self-knowledge, self-awareness, growth.	11.5
3. Peace of mind, emotional stability, lack of conflict; fear, anxiety; suffering, pain; humiliation, belittlement; escape, fantasy.	10.0
4. Sex, sexual satisfaction, sexual pleasure.	9.5
5. Challenge, stimulation; competition, competitiveness; ambition; opportunity, social mobility, luck; educational, intellectual stimulating.	8.0
6. Social acceptance, popularity; needed, feeling of being wanted; loneliness, impersonality; flattering, positive feedback, reinforcement.	8.0
7. Achievement, accomplishment, job satisfaction; success; failure, defeat, losing; money, acquisitiveness, material greed; status, reputation, recognition, prestige.	7.0
8. Individuality; conformity; spontaneity, impulsive, uninhibited; freedom.	6.0
9. Involvement, participation; concern, altruism, consideration.	6.0
10. Comfort, economic well-being, relaxation, leisure; good health.	6.0
11. Novelty, change, newness, variety, surprise; boredom; humorous, amusing, witty.	5.0
12. Dominance, superiority; dependence, impotence, helplessness; aggression, violence, hostility; power, control, independence.	3.5
13. Privacy.	2.0

Table 3-9
Rated EE Factors

	Relative Importance
1. Ability to learn, learning to learn; reasoning abilities, ability to think; critical ability, questioning, development of a critical attitude; synthesizing ability, a sense of organic relationship.	12.0
2. Broader outlook, new perspectives, scope, new experiences, exposing to new activities; knowledge; curiosity, desire to learn more.	10.0
3. Greater creativity, expanding the imagination, loss of creativity, loss of creative thinking.	8.0
4. Social awareness, awareness of others; awareness of environment, relationship of individual with environment; cultural awareness; social issues, awareness of societal problems.	8.0
5. Communication skill; relating to others; social contacts, opportunity to meet a variety of people; social skills, ability to get along with others.	7.0
6. Tolerance, decrease in prejudices; open-mindedness; understanding of others; narrowing of outlook, narrowing of values; liberalization of social and political views.	6.0
7. Self-awareness, increased self-understanding; honesty, personal integrity.	6.0
8. Self-confidence, self-reliance, independence; self-respect, self-acceptance, self-satisfaction; maturity, sexual maturity, more liberal sexual attitude.	6.0
9. Responsibility; concern for society, fellowman; political maturity, political awareness.	5.0
10. Impractical education, disillusionment with educational usefulness; irrelevancy, prescribed education, educational trivia.	5.0
11. Career skills, job competence; specialization, narrowing of interest to own field; elitism, social status.	5.0
12. Motivation, competitiveness; purpose in life, development of life goals.	5.0
13. Involvement, political involvement; isolation from real world, ivory-tower syndrome; dehumanization, repressive bureaucracy.	5.0
14. Loss of idealism, general dissatisfaction; political disillusionment.	1.0
15. Dependency, prolonged youth.	0.0

high for all four groups. The product-moment correlations between the median ratings on the first and second rounds is 0.99 for the QOL split-100 group, 0.97 for the QOL magnitude-estimation group, 0.97 for the EE split-100 group, and 0.99 for the EE 7-point rating scale group. The agreement between the rating methods for a given set of factors (reliability) is also very high. The plot of median magnitude estimation as a function of median split-100 rating for all the QOL factors is shown in figure 3-3. The open circles refer to the first round and the filled circles to the second. A similar graph for the EE factors is shown in figure 3-4; median 7-point rating is plotted as a function of median split-100 rating. Here again, the results for the first and second rounds are shown as open and filled circles, respectively. The correlation between the median (S-100) ratings and median magnitude-estimation ratings is 0.90 on the first round and 0.91 on the second for the QOL factors. The correlation between the median (S-100) and 7-point ratings for the EE factors is 0.88 on the first round and 0.93 on the second. Note that in both cases round two reliability was slightly greater than round one reliability.

The greatest change in group performance between rounds is the decrease in response variability from the first to the second round. Round two standard deviations (SD) are generally smaller than corresponding round one standard deviations, as is shown in tables 3-6 and 3-7. The statistical significance of this

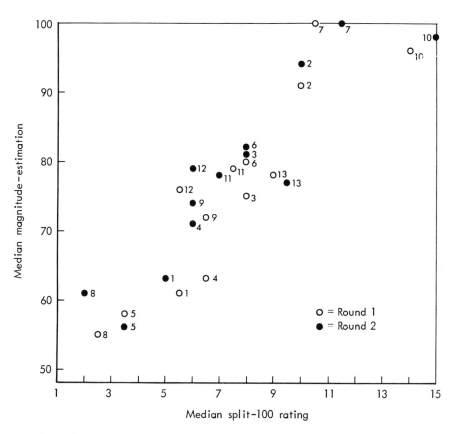

Figure 3-3. Cross-Plot of Split-100 and Magnitude-Estimation Median Ratings for QOL Factors.

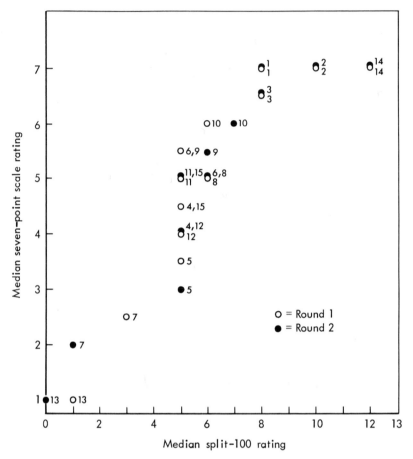

Figure 3–4. Cross-Plot of Split-100 and Seven-Point Scale Median Ratings for EE Factors.

decrease was assessed by comparing the mean of the SDs on the first round to the mean of the SDs on the second with t-tests.[6] The mean SDs were computed over the factors. The mean differences were in the expected direction for all four groups. Round one and round two differences are shown in table 3-10. Computed t's and significance levels (p) are also shown. All differences were reliable at least at the 0.01 level.

The distributions of the responses to the questions in the previous Delphi experiments have been bell shaped and generally positively skewed. In fact, the log-normal distribution has provided a very satisfactory fit to the observed distributions.[7] These distributions of importance ratings were not fit to the

Table 3-10

Differences between Round 1 and Round 2 Mean Standard Deviations for All Groups

Item	QOL S-100	QOL ME	EE S-100	EE 7-Point
SD_1-SD_2	0.45	4.0	0.75	0.34
t	3.03	7.34	4.58	7.59
df	12.00	12.00	14.00	14.00
p	<0.01	<0.005	<0.005	<0.005

log-normal distribution, but approximately equivalent bell-shaped distributions were expected for the ratings to each factor. In order to detect any deviant distributions, the following procedure was employed. First, the scores for each factor in each of the four groups were converted to deviation scores by subtracting the mean rating for a factor from each of the scores for the same factor. This centers the distributions of the ratings for all the factors about zero but does not change the variability, skewness, or kurtosis of the distributions. This transformed scale is used as the abscissa for figures 3-5, 3-6, and 3-7. Then the relative cumulative distribution for each factor was compared to the relative cumulative distribution for all the other factors combined in the same group and round with the Kolmogorov-Smirnov (K-S) two-sample test.[8] The tests were made on both the first- and second-round ratings within each of the groups; altogether 112 tests were conducted. Only four distributions were found which differed from the composite distributions at the 10-percent significance level. The composite distributions are shown in figure 3-5 for the second-round ratings for the QOL Split-100, QOL magnitude-estimation, EE Split-100, and EE 7-point rating scale groups. The curves are all bell shaped and generally skewed. The two most deviant distributions are shown in figure 3-6. Representative response distributions for the four groups on the second round are shown in figure 3-7. These were selected by choosing the response distribution within each group with the median p value according to the K-S tests.

Both groups of subjects (QOL and EE) rated the relevance of each EE factor to each of the QOL factors on a 0- to 3-point scale. Although the QOL group was more familiar with the QOL factors and the EE group with the EE factors, the relevance ratings from the two groups were in substantial agreement. The product-moment correlation between the two sets of ratings is 0.86. The mean ratings over the two groups combined are shown in table 3-11.

The EE to QOL relevance ratings and the importance ratings of the QOL factors were used to determine the contribution of each of the EE factors to the quality of life in the following manner. Let $e(i)$ be the contribution of the $i'th$ EE factor to the quality of life, let $r(i,j)$ be the relevance of the $i'th$ EE factor to the $j'th$ QOL factor, and let $q(j)$ be the importance of the $j'th$ QOL factor. The $e(i)$ were computed as

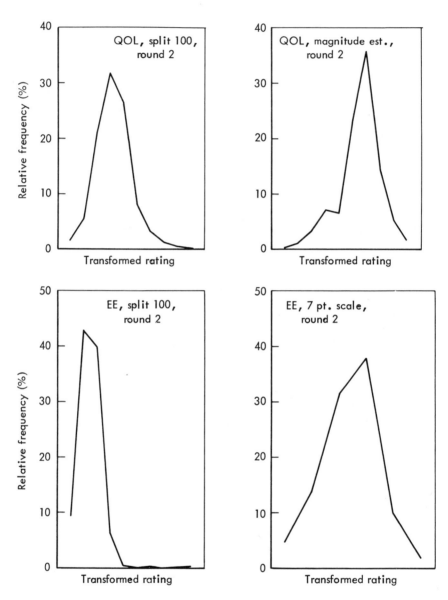

Figure 3-5. Average Frequency Distributions.

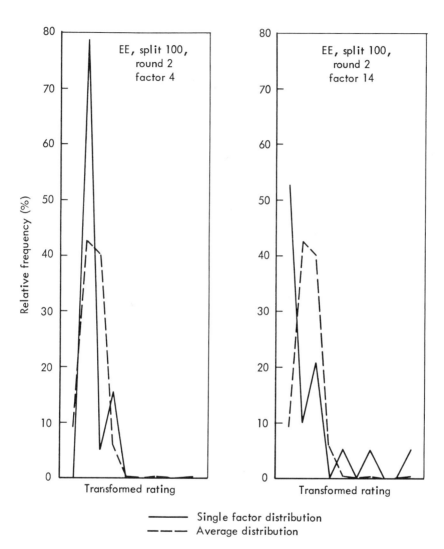

Figure 3-6. Most Deviant Distributions for Single Factors.

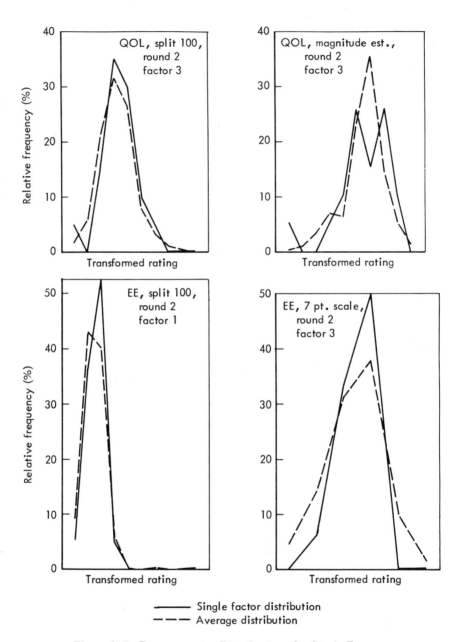

Figure 3-7. Representative Distributions for Single Factors.

Table 3-11
Combined Mean Relevance Ratings: QOL and EE Groups

EE Factors	Quality of Life Factors												
	1	2	3	4	5	6	7	8	9	10	11	12	13
1	2.671	1.566	1.237	1.118	1.131	2.250	1.803	0.671	1.171	1.421	1.776	2.447	1.473
2	2.592	1.790	1.513	1.171	1.013	2.303	2.210	0.579	1.947	1.895	1.526	2.211	1.631
3	1.618	1.671	2.158	0.973	1.289	1.895	2.026	0.539	2.671	2.395	1.236	1.750	1.185
4	0.947	1.395	1.315	2.065	1.855	2.000	1.763	0.579	1.105	0.645	2.724	1.145	0.315
5	1.224	1.447	1.750	1.053	1.724	1.539	1.447	0.869	2.474	1.487	1.500	1.487	0.737
6	1.145	2.434	1.895	1.369	1.368	1.527	2.855	1.197	1.605	2.448	1.250	2.276	2.053
7	0.776	1.408	1.013	0.671	1.381	1.000	1.039	0.658	1.394	0.934	1.118	0.948	0.408
8	1.500	2.368	1.947	1.645	1.566	1.895	2.750	1.105	1.777	2.461	1.750	2.250	2.500
9	1.737	1.816	1.750	1.013	1.237	1.447	2.039	0.474	2.171	2.289	1.158	1.948	1.408
10	1.816	1.803	2.605	1.382	1.671	1.724	1.987	0.803	2.342	2.552	1.645	1.684	1.803
11	1.079	1.342	1.671	1.039	1.184	1.618	1.776	0.619	2.566	2.026	1.263	1.421	0.881
12	1.276	1.684	1.473	1.763	1.829	2.566	2.066	0.671	1.473	1.171	2.461	1.526	0.921
13	0.644	1.461	1.289	1.040	1.750	0.843	1.184	0.895	0.724	1.053	1.013	1.092	0.974
14	2.013	1.632	1.316	1.224	1.158	2.289	2.131	0.763	1.474	1.632	1.921	1.829	1.039
15	0.750	1.131	0.685	0.711	1.092	1.250	0.855	0.421	0.723	0.500	1.079	0.724	0.250

$$e(i) = \sum_{j} r(i,j) \cdot q(j)$$

That is, the contribution of the *i'th* EE factor to the quality of life is the sum over all the QOL factors of the relevance of the *i'th* EE factor to the *j'th* QOL factor weighted by the importance of the *j'th* QOL factor.

A set of the "reweighted" EE factors was computed with the combined EE to QOL relevance ratings. The importance ratings of the QOL factors which were used in the computation were the round two medians from the QOL split-100 group. The reweighted EE factors are shown in table 3-12; the entries in the table have been normalized to sum to 100 and are listed in the same order as in table 3-9. The rank of each of the EE factors according to the reweighting is also given. The factor indices are keyed to the list of EE factors given in table 3-4.

Discussion

The results of applying the three criteria mentioned in the introduction to the ratings of the educational and quality of life factors are all favorable to the hypothesis that Delphi procedures are appropriate for formulating group value judgments. The results with value material are in general comparable with factual material. This comment, however, must be taken with a certain amount of

Table 3-12
Reweighted EE Factors

Factor (Listed as in Table 3-9)	Rank According to Reweighting	Reweighted Importance Ratings (sum = 100)
Ability to learn	7	7.0
Broader outlook	4	7.8
Creativity	9	6.9
Social awareness	5	7.6
Communication skills	3	8.4
Tolerance	6	7.3
Self-awareness	2	8.5
Self-confidence	1	9.1
Responsibility	10	6.5
Impractical education	15	3.3
Career skills	12	5.7
Motivation	8	7.0
Involvement	11	6.2
Loss of idealism	14	4.2
Dependency	13	4.6

caution. The variability of performance on factual questions is large, depending on the type of question, and it is not entirely clear what would be an appropriate population of factual questions to compare with the value judgments.

With this caveat in mind, some gross comparisons can be made: the correlations between the median split-100 ratings and magnitude-estimation ratings on the QOL factors is 0.90 on the first round; the correlation between the median split-100 and 7-point ratings for the EE factors is 0.88 on the first round. These compare with an average correlation of 0.85 for similar groups making factual estimates of general information.[9]

For the magnitude estimation and 7-point ratings of QOL and EE items respectively, convergence (variance reduction) occurred on all items in round two (tables 3-6 and 3-7). For split-100 ratings on the two sets of items, convergence occurred on all but two and three items respectively. For a set of eighty factual questions, convergence occurred in 97 percent of the cases. However, there is a difference in the amount of convergence. In a set of eight exercises involving short-range (three to nine month) predictions of "newsworthy" events, the average reduction in standard deviation was about 40 percent; for the value items in the present study, standard deviations decreased about 19 percent for magnitude-estimation and 7-point ratings and about 10 percent for split-100 ratings. It seems probable that the constraint of adding to 100 for split-100 ratings decreased the convergence, but still the variance reduction on feedback was about twice as great for factual questions.

With regard to distribution shape, the major feature to note is that all of the distributions for all rating methods were single peaked. In addition, only 4 distributions out of 112 failed the goodness of fit (to the average distribution) test at the 10-percent level. This compares very favorably with similar tests for eighty factual questions where roughly one-fourth of the cases failed the test of fit to an average distribution (log-normal) at the 10-percent level.

With respect to the number of changes of opinion between round one and round two, the proportion of those who changed their estimate varied from 34 percent for the EE group making 7-point ratings to 49 percent for the QOL group making magnitude-estimation ratings. This compares with 65-percent changes for four control groups (receiving only median and quartile feedback as in the present experiment) on factual questions.[10] The number of changes is lower for the value questions, but not so low as to reject the hypothesis that the subjects are responding to the feedback information.

Correlations were computed between the distance a subject's response was from the median on the first round, and the amount of change of the subject's response on the second round. These correlations are:

QOL, Split 100	0.40
QOL, Magnitude Estimation	0.41

| EE, Split 100 | 0.54 |
| EE, Magnitude Estimation | 0.44 |

No comparable correlations have been computed for the data on factual questions; however, these correlations appear to be in line with the result that for deviations from the mean of two quartiles, or less, the likelihood of a subject changing his estimate is roughly linear with deviation.

With the exception of the effects of iteration and feedback, the data generated by these experiments are similar to, and very much in line with, results obtained in a large number of experiments with psychophysical scaling, and with scaling subjective magnitudes. The subjective magnitude scaling experiments, in fact, can be interpreted as lending support to the general conclusion presented here. It is worth noting that the linear relationship between magnitude estimation and split-100 scaling indicated in figure 3-3 is in accord with the conclusion of S.S. Stevens that ratio scales are relatively easy to obtain for a wide variety of subjective magnitudes with group estimation.[11]

In the psychophysical and subjective magnitude studies, the role of the group judgment as opposed to individual judgments is left somewhat unclear. Stevens discusses the issue with respect to psychophysical judgments in terms of the similarity between individual intensity functions and group intensity functions. His assessment is that group judgments behave in the same general way as individual judgments. However, from the point of view of the present investigation, we are not so much concerned with the specific relationship of individual judgments to group, as we are to the assessment of the excellence of the group judgment. We take it for granted that individual judgments on both factual and value questions are based on incomplete, possibly biased, information; the general question, then, is to what extent pooling the judgments of a group of individuals is an improvement over the individual judgments. In the case of factual judgments of the sort studied in our experiments, the improvement is significant—overall group judgments were 45 percent more accurate than individual judgments. The present experiments (as well as the psychophysical ones) are compatible with the assumption that group judgments are, on the whole, more correct for subjective judgments.

The effects of iteration and feedback—reduction in variance on the second round, and changes in scale values—are apparently new phenomena in the field of subjective magnitude scaling and psychophysical experiments. But they are not completely foreign to a related field of research—the study of attitude change. There do not appear to have been any experiments in attitude research concerning the results of feedback of the simple sort we employed in the present experiments, but there is a large body of literature concerning what could be called feed-in of various kinds of material.[c] The focus of these experiments has

---

[c]We consider the experimental procedure employed by Asch[12] and others to be of this sort, although the information provided is generally misinformation; furthermore, the misinformation is presented so as to maximize the pressures towards conforming to the group response.

been more on the phenomenon of change in attitudes and its determinants than on the question whether (in some sense) the changed attitudes were improved. However, one general consideration coming out of these studies is directly relevant: by utilizing various sorts of feed-in, much larger changes than we obtained with the statistical feedback are easily obtained.

From the point of view of advancing the study of individual well-being or evaluation of higher education, these exercises should probably be considered exploratory. The list of quality-of-life factors is similar to, but not identical with lists that have been generated in other exercises using different groups of respondents and somewhat different aggregation techniques. Some of these are reported in chapter 4. The importance ratings are also similar to, but not identical with, importance ratings in the other exercises. Studies by Rokeach and others have shown that there are major differences in the ranking of terminal values depending upon income, education, and other characteristics of respondents.[13] There is no inconsistency between assuming a fair amount of stability for basic value categories and varying importance ratings on these categories for different life states, if it is assumed that tradeoffs between basic values are meaningful, and depend on the state of the individual in the QOL space (see chapter 4, "A Preliminary Model for the Analysis of Quality of Life"). However, the present exercise was not sufficiently rich to test this hypothesis, nor do we know of any studies that have examined the question.

Nevertheless, several suggestive results have emerged from the present study. The most interesting is the large disparity in rank order of educational categories obtained from direct ratings and the rank order derived from the weighted sum of judged contributions to the set of quality of life factors (table 3-12). The very large shifts—cognitive skills moving from rank 1 to rank 7, creativity from rank 3 to rank 9, self-confidence from rank 8 to rank 1, etc.—are certainly formally significant. The result suggests as an interesting hypothesis for further exploration that some of the present discontent with the university stems in part from a (perhaps fuzzy) perception of just this disparity on the part of many students.

Another suggestive result is the high rating students give to security and peace of mind. A well-worn comment in news media is that one trouble with students is they take affluence and security for granted, and thus are not firmly guided by the reality principle. These results would suggest perhaps the opposite is the case. Security is high in their list of values. Of course, the student judgments may concern a different conception of security than that envisaged by the news media.

4

Measurement and Analysis of the Quality of Life

Norman C. Dalkey, Ralph Lewis
and David Snyder

Introduction

The phrase *quality of life* has almost supplanted the older words *happiness* and *welfare* in contemporary discussions of policy in urban and domestic areas.[a] The phrase does have a fine ring to it and it is somewhat less maudlin than *happiness* and somewhat less clinical than *welfare*. However, it is debatable whether the new phrase is any less vague.

The expression is most often encountered as a slogan—a call to think bigger. There is nothing particularly objectionable in its hortatory use, except that the term is rarely defined and one suspects it contributes its bit of soot to the verbal smog. Most users are careful not to pause for definition, but hurry on to more operational problems, like setting performance goals.

In this report we have de-emphasized policy issues and have concentrated on the attempt to add content to the notion of quality of life. In addition, we have focused our attention on the quality of life of individual persons. From the standpoint of the policy maker, there are group interests that may transcend the interests of individual members of the group; but the issue of group versus individual values adds a tangle of conceptual problems that seemed expedient to sidestep for the time being.

There is another clarification to make before proceeding. The notion of *quality* has two aspects: it can refer to state or condition, or it can refer to excellence. The difference is probably subtle, and mainly semantic; but life becomes a little simpler if we start off with a descriptive, rather than a prescriptive, notion. This boils down to considering the aim to be a characterization of the factors that are relevant and important to the well-being of individuals, and not to prescribing what is socially good.

As you will observe, we tend to be rather bullish about the feasibility of getting somewhere in the attempt to make the notion of quality of life (QOL) useful to planners (as more than a handy slogan). Our reasons are fairly diffuse.

---

[a]"Our purpose in this period should not be simply better management of the programs of the past. The time has come for a new quest—a quest not for a greater quantity of what we have—but for a new quality of life in America." President Nixon's State of the Union address to Congress, January 22, 1970.

There is a small but growing body of information in psychology that is relevant; there have been several studies by social scientists that are applicable; and there is a fair amount of agreement among armchair thinkers on the factors that are significant. This is not a sufficient basis for optimism—but it is a little better than an excuse.

We remarked earlier that few users of the phrase QOL bother to define it; however, some have attempted to give content to the notion, and it is worth examining these characterizations.

These attempts have taken two forms: armchair "analyses" and public surveys.

The armchair approach generally consists of devising a list of general factors that are important to the QOL of an individual. Representative samples are to be found in Bauer,[1] Berelson,[2] Lynd,[3] and a report from Stanford Research Institute (SRI).[4] A kind of superarmchair procedure is that of the prestigious commission, most notably the 1960 President's Commission on National Goals.[5] Again, the output is a list of items deemed (in this case) most important for the well-being of the nation, and hence, derivatively, for the individual. The report of the President's Commission has become a sort of bible in the national area. One investigator, Wilson,[6] has used the list of goals as a structure to rank the fifty states in the order of the QOL they offer their residents.

The public survey approach is well represented by three investigations—those of Gurin et al.,[7] Bradburn,[8,9]. These are analyses of the results of extensive interviews with cross-sectional samples of the American public. Despite the somewhat *Reader's Digest* flavor lent these studies by their unabashed use of words like *happiness, feelings,* and so forth, they have the virtue that they at least ask the relevant questions, rather than impose a priori assumptions.

Armchair Efforts

As noted above, the armchair approach consists of devising a list of general factors that are presumed to be significant in determining the well-being of humans. The lists referred to are, of course, not capricious. They are distilled from clinical lore, sociological think pieces, some psychological and social psychological experimentation, and the like. There is a great deal of overlap among the lists—in general, the shorter lists tend to be contained in the longer ones. The shortest list we have run across is that of SRI, which involves three basic factors: safety, belongingness, and self-esteem. A fourth item is appended, self-realization, but this is treated on a different level from the basic three.

The oldest list of this genre we have run across is dated 1923—in Berelson's *Human Behavior*, p. 257—and is next to the shortest. It includes a factor called "new experience." We prepared a list, semiindependent of the ones mentioned, and suppose it is only fair to use it as another example. The list contains nine items: health, activity, freedom, security, novelty, status, sociality, affluence, and aggression.

Strictly physiological items such as food, sleep, shelter, etc., have been omitted primarily on the grounds that, in the United States at least, these are generally taken care of at better than subsistence levels.

A number of misgivings arise at once concerning any attempt to set down a list of the significant factors in the QOL. The lists are intended to be comprehensive, but the varying lengths of those in the literature indicate there is no trustworthy stop rule for the multiplication of items. Again, the items are presumably distinct, but there is no good way of telling whether they overlap, or in fact, refer to the same thing. Finally, the items are extremely difficult to relate, on the one hand, to human behavior and, on the other, to policy.

In an attempt to introduce a somewhat more systematic treatment (but still within the armchair tradition) several exploratory exercises were conducted.

The first (1967) used twelve members of the Rand staff as a panel. They were asked to make judgments with respect to the nine factors given above. Specifically, the respondents were asked whether the qualities identified were (a) meaningful, (b) measurable, and (c) what relative weight would be assigned to each of these qualities by the average American.[b] They were also asked to add any new factors they thought were significant.

There was good agreement that the items were meaningful and good agreement that all were measurable except for freedom, novelty, and aggression. There was considerable diversity in the assignment of relative weights, but reasonable agreement on the rankings. The median relative weights, normalized to add up to 100, for the nine factors in QOL are as follows:

Factor	Median Weight
1. Health	20
2. Status	14
3. Affluence	14
4. Activity	12.25
5. Sociality	9.8
6. Freedom	8.2
7. Security	8.2
8. Novelty	7.2
9. Aggression	6.1

As can be seen, the items break up into three main groups: (1) health, (2) status, affluence, activity, (3) sociality, freedom, security, novelty, and aggression.

How much these results reflect the Rand environment is difficult to determine. We had intended to pursue the exercise for at least another round, feeding back the results of the first round to the panel for further consideration,

---

[b]The questionnaire used for this exercise is included as appendix A.

but decided against it, since no procedure suggested itself for dealing with either the overlap or the completeness problem.

The only two items suggested for addition by more than one member of the panel were sexual activity and care of children (including education).

The second exercise was conducted using twelve European scholars (mostly from universities) attending a conference on The Dialogue (Spring 1968) at the Center for the Study of Democratic Institutions at Santa Barbara, California. The exercise was addressed to the expected change in QOL in Europe and North America over the next twenty-five years and the major factors influencing that change. There was good agreement that QOL would improve moderately during the quarter-century (and improve greatly in the socialist countries). The major factors responsible for change were listed (in order of rated importance) as (1) scientific-technological revolution, (2) increased standard of living, (3) increased level of education, (4) other, (5) increased public attention to human values, (6) increased international exchange and communication, (7) armaments race—increased armaments, (8) political tensions, (9) increased dehumanization and satiety, (10) increased secularization of life, (11) loosening of family structure.

"Other" was a miscellaneous collection of items such as population increase, increased leisure, democratization of socialist states, and so on. It was included to indicate that all respondents thought some other factor than the named ones would be relatively important. Except for science-technology, which most respondents thought would have both positive and negative effects, the items through (6) were considered to be positive, and those below negative; i.e., the more important elements were construed in an optimistic fashion. There was not sufficient time to explore the question of whether there was a bias introduced by a tendency to consider first the positive items and then the negative ones.

The third exercise was conducted with a small number of students from California Polytechnic Institute (spring 1968). They filled out both the questionnaires used with the Rand group and the one used at the Center for the Study of Democratic Institutions. On the rating of qualities, they gave an entirely different set of weights than the Rand group—with freedom on the top and affluence (income) near the bottom. Whether this represented a "generation gap" between the two groups, or more simply reflected the special culture of the university environment, was not clear. The responses on the change in QOL over the next quarter-century and the factors accounting for it were very similar to the European group except for armaments and the arms race, which did not appear in the students' list.

The fourth exercise was conducted with a limited number of graduate student consultants to Rand (Summer 1968). The exercise was somewhat more ambitious than the preceding. The subjects were asked to devise independently a list of factors that they considered important in QOL. After minor editing, a "raw" list of about thirty factors remained. The subjects were then asked to weight these factors by a voting procedure that enabled the selection of the most representative factors. The nine selected were: novelty, freedom, self-esteem, sense of accomplishment, physical activity-exercise, security, sociality, expression of feeling, physical impact.

Although these exercises have been on much too small a scale to produce substantive results, they have indicated that procedures are feasible for eliciting opinions concerning both the factors of QOL and their relative weights. Enough diversity in opinions has shown up in these limited investigations to suggest that in the population as a whole there is a wide range of judgments as to what is and what is not important in QOL. The effect of feedback is apparent, and there is sufficient indication that convergence of opinions attendant on feedback represents a "true" shift of opinion to warrant making this phenomenon a major item of study.

General Considerations

Without a good deal more empirical study than now exists, the armchair lists are probably only suggestive. However, they are in agreement on one general proposition: Whatever QOL is, it is determined mainly by some very general features of the individual and his environment, and not by specifics. What this means is that two different individuals who score about the same on a QOL scale should, for example, report about the same degree of contentment with their lot, irrespective of the special circumstances that make up the score. This is a very strong statement. Providing the factors are measurable, it is testable, and one of the problems to be tackled is how we can go about testing it.

An important issue is whether we are looking for a single thing that can be called QOL, or whether we presume it is a congeries of incomparable elements. Several levels are possible here: If we consider the factors to be—as Lynd([3]) does—motivations, or forces, we can ask whether there are tradeoffs among them. If so, there is a reasonable sense in which "equi-motivating" curves can be drawn and a general "desirability" index defined. A somewhat different notion is involved in using terms such as *happiness* to describe an overall feeling-tone to which the various status variables contribute. A third point of view is that of the mental hygienist that apparently would include some notion of the effectiveness of the individual, as well as his feeling-tone.

In the present discussion, we vacillate among the three. Our inclinations are to favor the mental hygiene approach, but the difficulties of implementing this in system analyses of domestic problems nudge us toward the simpler structures.

In addition to the very general postulate that QOL is determined by some highly abstract properties of the living space of the individual, there are two other propositions that seem to be supported by a fair amount of evidence. The first is that the influences of individual factors of QOL are a rapidly decreasing function of distance, either in space or time. The statement with respect to time is very similar to the notion of discount rate in economics. The opportunity of obtaining a dollar one year from now is much less motivating than the opportunity to obtain a dollar this afternoon. With regard to space, there has been a fairly rich experimental program with animals, and especially with rats, that demonstrates the properties of what psychologist Clark L. Hull has called the "goal gradient."[10] If any of several indicators of motivation are employed (how rapidly the rat runs toward a goal, the physical tug the rat exerts against a restraint, as measured by a harness and a spring balance, etc.), the general relationship of this measure and distance from the goal is that of an exponential decrease as shown in figure 4-1.

One of the most beautiful sets of experiments in all psychology demonstrates the interaction of positive and negative goal gradients.[11] In a given name, the positive goal gradient, e.g., for food, can be measured. Suppose for the same maze, a negative goal gradient is measured, e.g., for an electric shock. The curve will again look like figure 4-1, except that, of course, the effect is a push away from the goal rather than a tug. Now, suppose the rat is faced with a situation where there is food and an electric shock at the goal position. It appears to be the case that the decline of the negative force is more rapid than the decline of the positive force; hence, the two curves will cross, as in figure 4-2. The remarkable thing is that although the two curves were measured independently, when the goal is mixed, the rat will approach the goal until he reaches the crossover point and then stop. If he is placed closer to the goal than the crossover point, he will retreat to the crossover and again stop. If he is placed precisely at the crossover, he will remain there. In short, the reality of the equality of the push and the tug is elegantly borne out.

Probably even for rats, but certainly for humans, the goal gradient would need modification in terms of psychological distance, as well as physical distance, although it is striking that sheer physical distance appears to be a factor in many psychological and sociological phenomena. In particular, Zipf has found some surprising relationships between distance and social interactions, such as

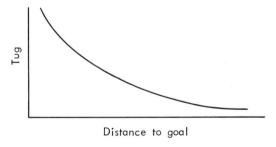

Distance to goal

Figure 4-1. Exponential Decrease of Positive Force.

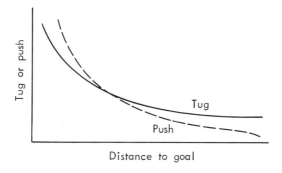

Figure 4-2. Relative Decline of Positive and Negative Force.

the sharp inverse dependence of frequency of marriage on distance between couples' residences.[12]

The other general proposition is that human beings live much more "in the future" than lower animals. Hope, anticipation, ambition, aspiration level, anxiety, etc., are clearly important elements of QOL. But it seems reasonable to assume that events of the distant future are much less influential than near events. It also seems reasonable that the "discount rate" depends on the kind of event and the degree of uncertainty surrounding it. We are not aware of any experiments in which the timewise goal gradient for animals has been systematically investigated, but it looks like a tractable subject.

Surveys

A somewhat more empirical approach is furnished by the cross-sectional survey. The three studies, *Americans View Their Mental Health* (1960), *Reports on Happiness* (1966), and *The Structure of Psychological Well-Being* are among the more complete and recent such surveys. Lengthy interviews—of the order of two hours involving over a hundred questions—were held with representative samples of the U.S. population. Questions ranged from the subjective and global ("Taking all things together, how would you say things are these days?" "Would you say you're very happy, pretty happy, or not too happy?") to the objective and specific ("About what do you think your total income will be this year for yourself and your immediate family?").

Such surveys are subject to a host of well-known objections. These were recognized by the investigators, but, of course, are hard to deal with. It is difficult to check the reliability of verbal reports; they are hard to relate to behavior; subjective evaluations are likely to exhibit bias and cultural distortion, and so on. In addition, the survey approach has very little in the way of conceptual framework to suggest hypotheses and structure the results.

Nevertheless, the survey results are not empty. For one thing, they over-turned several well-entrenched bits of popular sociology. A good example is the myth of the carefree bachelor. Standard lore has it that the single man enjoys his freedom, while the single woman is anxiously awaiting the loss of hers. Something like the opposite appears to be the case. The unmarried male is much more likely to rate himself as "not very happy" than the unmarried female, independent of age.

An interesting result from the *Reports on Happiness* study is that successions of events, some with positive and some with negative feeling tones, do not smear into an intermediate shade of emotional gray, but make distinct contributions to a self-evaluation. Persons reporting being very or pretty happy are likely to report a greater number of both unpleasant and pleasant events in the recent past than those reporting being not very happy.

For those interested in urban affairs, the surveys raise somewhat of a puzzle. In comparing self-evaluations of urban and rural dwellers, no measurable difference could be found when respondents were matched for other obvious variables—age, sex, education, income, married or not. Admittedly, the measuring stick was crude, but at least the other variables mentioned did make a distinct difference.

A Preliminary Model for the Analysis of Quality of Life

The following model for analysis of QOL is presented as a preliminary structure to guide empirical investigations. It is not to be considered either complete or particularly exact, but it does seem to have enough substance to suggest fruitful types of data collection and analysis, or, we hope, even experimentation.

To a first approximation, *life* can be considered as a sequence of events in time occurring to an individual. The division into events is partially an arbitrary one, partially a simple commonsense observation that sequences of occurrences (perceptual, behavioral) are ordinarily divided into more or less coherent units, somewhat as the perceived environment is divided into objects—taking a bath, going through a marriage ceremony, eating dinner, etc. It seems very likely that the usual way a person breaks down the stream of occurrences into events is conditioned by a host of cultural factors, but also, we might presume, it is partly determined by the basic neurological organization. For the purpose of this study, it is not necessary to examine the precise wellsprings of the resolution into events or to take careful cognizance of the fact that events can be nested or overlapping.

As a first approximation, it would appear that an event can last just seconds or up to several hours. Certainly the span of an event is longer than what used to be called the "specious present"—the perceived "now." As a first approximation below, "now" will be assumed to extend over any event that is occurring at the reference time.

An event is assumed to be characterized (among other things) by a number of properties to be called *qualities* that are scalable, and that are directly relevant to the QOL of the individual. These qualities need not be apparent to the individual, but some may be. However, perceived or not, it is assumed that the location of the event in the quality space determines its contribution to the well-being of the individual.

A highly preliminary list of these qualities would include novelty, freedom, affluence, status, sociality, health (how "good" one feels), meaningful activity, and aggression.

In addition to the qualities of individual events, it is assumed there are a number of aspects of the "now" that play a role in the QOL of the individual. The structure of these additional features is less precise than the qualities. They appear to be "second level" items that are concerned with the trajectory through the quality space. Among these are: security, expectation, and level of aspiration.

If, for the moment, we assume that 1 through 8 can be expressed as a single magnitude, Q, the life of the individual is represented as a fluctuating pattern of Q over time, where the future pattern has several differences from the past, as shown in figure 4-3. In particular, the future contains a set of potential trajectories that clearly grows broader for a while but may coalesce (e.g., at a time beyond which death is practically certain). This construct has major difficulties—in particular, it is not clear how the future pattern actually is represented in most individual minds. It is at least a quite fuzzy notion for most normal situations. It is probably very spotty and extremely incomplete. However, for most of the following, making the notion more precise will probably not lose the important properties.

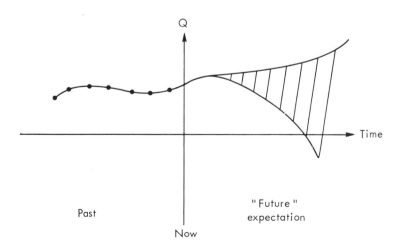

Figure 4-3. Fluctuating Pattern of Q Over Time.

We can define *expectation* as either the totality of the perceived set of future paths, with an attendant weight function over the set, or as some representative path (e.g., the expected path in the statistical sense). Security may be just the expectation (an expected path that remains high is secure) or it may be some measure of the perceived likelihood of a disastrous path.

It can be postulated that some form of discounting should be applied to events both in the past and in the future, to take into account a decreasing influence of more distant events. The discount rate would determine, for example, the practical span of events that would be examined to assess the QOL level for an individual. Paradoxically, this notion is clearer for the past than for the future. Although there is no doubt that present expectations have a strong effect on perceived well-being, there is a perfectly reasonable sense in which expectations can be said to be determined by the sequence of events up to now, and therefore, in order to predict the QOL rating of an individual, all that need be looked at is the sequence in the past.

The role of aspiration level is similarly ambiguous. There appears to be no doubt that, at one stage of abstraction, aspiration level plays an important role in determining the significance of the future projection for an individual. At another stage of abstraction, however, the aspiration level can be considered a function of the preceding sequence of events and hence is not required. However, it appears that aspiration level may be a very complex function of the sequence and, since it may be measured more directly, it may permit a major simplification. If so, the whole apparatus of expectations, future discounts, etc., would also be useful.

Which of these various interpretations is most useful will have to be established by some form of semiempirical investigations. The word "semi-empirical" is used because at first, probably, the only way to get at this problem is to ask people. After a sufficiently sharp set of concepts has been established,[c] more quantitative types of investigation can be envisaged.

In addition to the set of qualities that characterize events and determine the contributions of events to the QOL of the individual, there is assumed to be a set of properties attached to the individual at a given time that can be called "determiners." (In more usual terminology, I suppose these would be called independent variables and, in this context, the qualities would be called dependent variables; but there are several levels here, and besides, the model is not yet complete enough to warrant the implied precision of the independent-dependent variable language.)

Determiners are properties of the individual such as income, socioeconomic status, education, health, etc., that have the following characteristics: (1) they

---

[c]The degree of sharpness required here may not be especially high for useful investigations. The scales of positive and negative feelings, and the scale of sociality used in the NORC (note 9) studies of happiness are relatively crude, and yet they appear to enable meaningful relationships to be determined.

are relatively stable compared with the qualities, i.e., they change more slowly and usually more continuously; (2) they are more "objective" in that most of them can be measured fairly well; and (3) they are relatively more controllable in terms of public policy.

The basic assumption concerning this set is that they determine to a great extent the qualities; or, in other words, given the location of an individual in the determiner space, a relatively reliable prediction can be made concerning the nature of the stream of events occurring to the individual. Finding out how they determine the nature of events is, in part, a matter of research strategy. One fairly complex model postulates that they operate by fixing an opportunity region in event space, and the individual has relatively free choice within this region. A possible assumption relevant to the notion of qualities is that there are tradeoff curves (see figure 4-4) determining the relative contribution of each quality (at a point) to the overall well-being of the individual. Assuming the individual operates rationally, he will choose a point that maximizes his QOL. It is not necessary, however, to assume that the individual is rational to make use of this model.

A somewhat simpler model assumes that there is a statistical function that maps the D space onto the Q space. This approach is used by most investigators in the sociology of happiness. For some purposes, it may give more useful insights than the choice model.

Not included in the qualities model are the behavioral consequences of given levels of well-being. The model, as it stands, does assume that the payoff in an individual's life can be expressed in QOL units. Whether a low QOL is associated with dissatisfaction and hence with behavior tending to increase satisfaction, or a

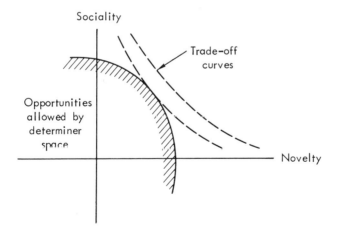

Figure 4-4. Interaction of Determiners and Events.

high QOL associated with satisfaction and thus with behavior tending to maintain the status quo, is not a part of the structure. Such considerations can, of course, be added as separate empirical relationships.

The choice model, more completely formulated, would have behavioral implications. This is the case whether the model is formulated in terms of rational choice or in terms of some more empirically defined form of choice behavior. However, not enough data exists to warrant exploring these implications here.

A Delphi Investigation of the Quality of Life Models

Respondents

This exercise involved four feedback rounds, with twenty-four respondents—fourteen graduate students and ten federal mid-career executives in an administration program. Only two of the respondents were women, which implies a possible bias (also present in previous exercises). In the future, we hope to obtain a more representative set of respondents. Since subjects were asked to respond to questions by answering how they thought others (people in general) viewed the QOL (i.e., they were asked to be experts on people), the procedure is hopefully less biased by the composition of the sample population than other techniques such as surveys or inventories that ask people about their own individual preferences.

Introductory Material. A meeting including a description of the Delphi process and some general comments on the QOL was conducted with the respondents before beginning the exercise. In this verbal summary, no specific information on the characteristics thought to be involved in an individual's QOL or the weights of such characteristics were discussed.

The instructions were summarized in writing before the first round and began as follows:

This is the first in a series of (four) questionnaires dealing with the identification, weighting, and interactions of the factors determining the quality of life of individuals. The phrase "quality of life" is vague, as are similar global terms—happiness, psychological well-being, the good life, positive mental health, etc. This is an attempt to clarify the phrase. It is part of a continuing research project involving several different approaches to the evaluation of individual well-being.

Most, if not all, individuals in western society carry on an intermittent, but relatively frequent, process of self-evaluation. A sort of "Where do I stand?" running score. With different individuals it is done to varying degrees of explicitness, combined with equally varying amounts of conscious planning. Most respondents, when asked the question: "Taking things all together, how would you say things are these days—would you say you are *very happy, pretty happy,* or *not too happy?*" will come up with an answer. The responses furnish repeatable correlations with a number of demographic indices—education, health, age, income, marital status. The basis for the response, whether a conscious evaluation, or a report of a "feeling tone," has not been established by the national surveys asking the question, but reasonable interrelationships have been found for a simple index of positive and negative experiences during the previous week and the reported level of happiness.

The following questions explore some of the properties of the individual's self-evaluation. In making your responses, rely on first general impressions. There will be an opportunity to revise your answers on succeeding rounds.

The following instructions were given at the beginning of the second round describing the format for the majority of the items that would be returned to the group of reevaluation. The responses shown in this report also follow these conventions.

In the attached items you will find the group response from the previous round. In those questions where a numerical estimate was requested, the median and quartiles of the distribution of answers are reported in the format: LOWER QUARTILE/MEDIAN/UPPER QUARTILE.

The median is the mid-answer and the two quartiles enclose 50 percent of the answers.

On those questions that required only concurrence with a particular item, the reported group response is the number of responses on that item.

General Questions about the Nature of the Quality of Life. The first question dealt with the existence of self-evaluation in the life of individuals.

What proportion of the adult population—18 years old and over—maintain some form of running evaluation, explicit or implicit, of themselves or of their "life"?

Lower Quartile	Median	Upper Quartile
80%	85%	91%

It appears that the majority of the respondents agreed that some evaluation is kept by most persons. The second question, however, suggests that the score is not explicitly kept by a large number of persons.

What proportion of those who "keep score" do so explicitly?

Lower Quartile	Median	Upper Quartile
5%	20%	40%

Since there appeared to be a large spread of opinion on this question, the same question was fed back in the following round, resulting in a minor degree of convergence.

What proportion of those who "keep score" do so explicitly?

Lower Quartile	Median	Upper Quartile
10%	20%	40%

Content of a Quality-of-Life Index. The following questions were asked:

In general, how is the score kept? (Indicate proportion for each type.)

a. In an overall "index"—how happy, how well things are going, etc.

First Round			Feedback Round		
Lower Quartile	Median	Upper Quartile	Lower Quartile	Median	Upper Quartile
10%	20%	32%	15%	20%	27%

b. In terms of more specific items—such as not too good in some respects— pretty good in other respects.

First Round			Feedback Round		
Lower Quartile	Median	Upper Quartile	Lower Quartile	Median	Upper Quartile
10%	15%	20%	10%	15%	20%

c. Mainly in terms of "what's wrong."

First Round			Feedback Round		
Lower Quartile	Median	Upper Quartile	Lower Quartile	Median	Upper Quartile
5%	20%	30%	15%	25%	30%

d. Mainly in terms of a general feeling tone or state of satisfaction or dissatisfaction.

First Round			Feedback Round		
Lower Quartile	Median	Upper Quartile	Lower Quartile	Median	Upper Quartile
17%	30%	50%	20%	32%	45%

e. Other—specify.

Feedback Round: Four responses given below.

o Two responses that indicated the score was kept (20%, 5%) in terms of peer group norms or standards.
o One response that indicated the score was kept (10%) in terms of what others thought of one's happiness.
o One response that indicated the score was kept (10%) in terms of a fairly thorough and honest appraisal of factors responsible for the score.

It appears that the score is kept in a plurality of fashions. There was very high concurrence on the fact that however the score was kept, if asked how happy an individual was—as has been done on a number of public surveys—the response would be a report of the individual's "running score."

When a respondent in a national survey states his level of happiness is either *very happy, pretty happy,* or *not too happy,* is this equivalent to a report of his running score?

No. of Responses

20   a. Yes, his answer is a measure of his running score, or
4   b. No, that question is not a measure of his running score.

Components of the Quality-of-Life Index

A major emphasis was placed in these exercises on developing a comprehensive structure of the QOL index as perceived by the respondents. Using a question similar to one previously used, the respondents were asked to describe characteristics that influence the QOL in the United States.

Using the form (shown below) entitled "Characteristics," answer the following:

a. Drawing on both your own experience and your experience with other people, give a list of those characteristics of events that you believe to have the strongest influence on the quality of life of an adult American. (For this exercise we will not raise the issue of whether or not the factors are strongly culture-dependent.) Accompany each characteristic with a short definition or set of synonyms. List at least five such characteristics, but no more than ten.
b. For each characteristic, indicate whether it can generate both positive and negative effects, or only one of these.

CHARACTERISTICS LIST

Characteristics of Events	Definitions or Synonyms	Effect	
		+	—

Approximately 125 individual characteristics were reported. Many of these were very similar. The 125 characteristics were aggregated by the staff into the 38 separate items shown in table 4-1. It was felt that 38 items were still too many for a reasonable, workable model.

On the second round, the 38 items were fed back to the respondents with the instructions:

In the attached matrix you will find a summary of the "qualities" list from the first round. In the process of editing the responses from the first round of the questionnaire, we omitted those items that describe basic biological needs such as minimal food, hunger, basic shelter, etc. In some cases, both desirable and undesirable characteristics that describe the same underlying characteristics appeared in the collected list. These would be typified by such items as rejection/social acceptance, boredom/excitement. In such cases, only descriptors for one end of the continuum are included in the edited list.

In Part II of this questionnaire, we would like to investigate your opinion of how interdependent these qualities are. Using the scale shown below, will you please indicate the degree of relationship between the different characteristics on the attached matrix. For purposes of simplifying this task, assume that the relationships are symmetric—that is, whatever relationship holds between characteristics A and B also holds between B and A, so that only one half of the matrix needs to be filled out.

Using the code (0, 1, 2, 3, 4) shown below, indicate on the attached matrix the relationships between all different pairs of characteristics. If one characteristic is related to another but in a negative or opposite way,[d] place a line below the number, e.g.,

	Hate	
Love	3	

---

[d]After looking at the responses, we found a number of low relationships on items that were negative with respect to the majority of the items (e.g., aggression, dominance). Possibly items such as these elicit a low rating because they are negative.

Table 4-1
Aggregated Interdependency Ratings

Thirty-Eight Aggregated Characteristics[a]	Relax	Playful	Humorous	Satisfy	Privacy	Intimacy	Comfort	Physical	Pleasure	Depression	Marital	Aesthetic	Personal	Spirit	Novelty	Exciting	Freedom	Aggression	Security	New	Innovate	Meaning	Material	Educate	Planned	Charity	Esteem	Job set	Equality	Evaluate	Control	Business	Accomplishment	Accepted	Dominant	Historic	Status	Sexual
Relaxation—easing, recreation, leisure, rest (24)	0	28	24	18	39	25	36	28	15	22	10	24	11	15	24	8	26	5	15	6	19	11	13	10	13	18	6	11	10	12	10	5	4	5	6	5	6	25
Playfulness—fun (20)	0	0	31	25	28	28	44	32	18	27	11	12	12	14	18	19	12	4	4	25	7	10	11	8	6	16	8	14	8	6	12	4	7	14	5	3	5	29
Humorous (22)	0	0	18	5	9	13	7	16	24	30	16	16	11	8	11	19	8	10	10	7	11	13	5	8	4	16	2	15	5	4	5	9	5	11	7	1	3	11
Satisfying to the senses—warm, physical pleasure (7)	0	0	0	20	28	37	40	44	32	16	24	13	16	20	17	12	6	20	4	11	7	15	5	10	10	14	8	6	20	5	9	11	11	6	5	13	48	
Privacy—withdrawn from social visibility (1)	0	0	0	0	37	26	13	26	15	32	17	32	25	8	10	7	7	18	15	11	25	13	5	10	10	14	9	9	4	18	9	8	15	7	1	12	29	
Intimacy—affection, friendship, closeness, tenderness (34)	0	0	0	0	0	24	17	23	29	44	24	37	19	7	18	8	7	18	5	8	25	8	14	4	14	14	8	11	10	7	4	8	18	2	7	13	50	
Comfort (6)	0	0	0	0	0	0	39	41	23	30	10	26	26	7	7	13	14	26	7	6	11	31	22	8	20	20	24	14	10	12	5	8	21	7	13	13	32	
Physical well-being—health, feeling good and "alive" (12)	0	0	0	0	0	0	0	38	30	15	11	15	15	7	18	8	9	24	11	14	9	19	7	12	14	20	15	14	7	18	12	19	11	6	6	13	37	
Pleasurable—satisfying, feeling of contentment (4)	0	0	0	0	0	0	0	0	19	31	30	12	15	5	19	18	9	29	3	14	17	23	10	14	11	15	25	7	14	16	13	19	11	13	9	14	48	
Depression—sorrow, grief, tragedy (11)	0	0	0	0	0	0	0	0	0	20	10	18	30	11	27	24	24	10	7	9	12	11	10	11	18	27	7	21	17	12	12	25	7	7	7	12	18	
Marital satisfaction (35)	0	0	0	0	0	0	0	0	0	0	10	39	16	11	20	16	15	21	10	4	29	14	22	8	21	9	10	14	13	12	12	18	14	15	6	14	52	
Aesthetic surroundings (25)	0	0	0	0	0	0	0	0	0	0	0	11	25	9	9	15	6	8	7	10	14	12	14	9	21	11	13	15	6	12	14	18	14	15	9	12	18	
Personal—the event is shared by a few people (32)	0	0	0	0	0	0	0	0	0	0	0	0	25	8	11	7	8	16	6	8	19	11	11	5	19	7	15	9	16	9	12	13	4	7	7	8	31	
Spiritual serenity—inspiration, oneness with God (23)	0	0	0	0	0	0	0	0	0	0	0	0	0	8	11	11	6	19	8	1	11	10	11	11	5	11	13	16	14	12	14	18	7	14	9	11	15	
Novelty—surprising, unanticipated, unexpected (26)	0	0	0	0	0	0	0	0	0	0	0	0	0	0	27	7	12	10	36	25	29	10	15	16	25	24	14	16	14	16	13	13	11	11	16	12	15	
Exciting—stimulating, arousing (27)	0	0	0	0	0	0	0	0	0	0	0	0	0	0	0	12	8	7	35	36	19	8	16	25	24	14	14	16	18	17	18	14	20	7	7	6	18	
Freedom—lack of restraints lack of compulsion (9)	0	0	0	0	0	0	0	0	0	0	0	0	0	0	0	0	11	23	0	22	13	11	19	13	5	17	22	11	11	17	14	14	10	7	1	5	43	
Aggression—interpersonal conflict, blowing off steam (38)	0	0	0	0	0	0	0	0	0	0	0	0	0	0	0	0	0	13	7	26	13	21	11	8	17	4	14	11	11	4	5	16	2	12	4	12	25	
Security—safety, as opposed to anxious us or threatened (10)	0	0	0	0	0	0	0	0	0	0	0	0	0	0	0	0	0	0	10	10	9	33	14	13	20	22	25	26	13	18	27	18	15	25	14	25	21	
New—unfamiliar, strange (37)	0	0	0	0	0	0	0	0	0	0	0	0	0	0	0	0	0	0	0	22	21	0	22	29	16	25	28	1	14	8	21	5	14	6	5	6	3	
Innovative—creative (21)	0	0	0	0	0	0	0	0	0	0	0	0	0	0	0	0	0	0	0	0	21	0	27	25	16	21	23	20	25	7	22	21	11	11	21	18	31	
Meaningfulness—importance, sincerity, genuineness, usefulness (36)	0	0	0	0	0	0	0	0	0	0	0	0	0	0	0	0	0	0	0	0	0	21	9	27	12	16	21	21	25	7	21	22	21	16	18	31		
Material well-being—affluence, material comforts (18)	0	0	0	0	0	0	0	0	0	0	0	0	0	0	0	0	0	0	0	0	0	0	8	25	18	32	9	18	28	29	34	13	6	32	7			
Educational—one learns something from the event (33)	0	0	0	0	0	0	0	0	0	0	0	0	0	0	0	0	0	0	0	0	0	0	0	11	14	16	11	14	16	31	10	20	8	16	16	13	33	17
Planned for—anticipated, scheduled (8)	0	0	0	0	0	0	0	0	0	0	0	0	0	0	0	0	0	0	0	0	0	0	0	0	9	16	17	18	26	17	27	9	8	17	28	13	11	16
Charity—humanitarian, satisfaction of helping others (13)	0	0	0	0	0	0	0	0	0	0	0	0	0	0	0	0	0	0	0	0	0	0	0	0	0	29	11	11	29	11	10	8	11	16	11	12	12	8
Self-esteem—ego satisfying, pride, self-image (16)	0	0	0	0	0	0	0	0	0	0	0	0	0	0	0	0	0	0	0	0	0	0	0	0	0	0	32	13	26	32	31	42	21	29	20	18	34	
Job satisfaction—job motivation, enjoyment of work (17)	0	0	0	0	0	0	0	0	0	0	0	0	0	0	0	0	0	0	0	0	0	0	0	0	0	0	0	12	27	27	33	38	21	26	14	13	11	5
Equality—justice (29)	0	0	0	0	0	0	0	0	0	0	0	0	0	0	0	0	0	0	0	0	0	0	0	0	0	0	0	0	12	17	27	7	9	8	17	28	11	5
Evaluative—brings feedback or environmental awareness (5)	0	0	0	0	0	0	0	0	0	0	0	0	0	0	0	0	0	0	0	0	0	0	0	0	0	0	0	0	0	17	25	28	14	7	29	18	12	
Control—directness, under one's own power (30)	0	0	0	0	0	0	0	0	0	0	0	0	0	0	0	0	0	0	0	0	0	0	0	0	0	0	0	0	0	0	22	22	16	36	9	24	12	
Business esteem—job progress, success in work (19)	0	0	0	0	0	0	0	0	0	0	0	0	0	0	0	0	0	0	0	0	0	0	0	0	0	0	0	0	0	0	0	32	33	23	11	24	4	
Accomplishment—achievement, meeting goals, success (15)	0	0	0	0	0	0	0	0	0	0	0	0	0	0	0	0	0	0	0	0	0	0	0	0	0	0	0	0	0	0	0	0	32	14	27	27	25	
Social acceptance—belonging, recognition by peer group (14)	0	0	0	0	0	0	0	0	0	0	0	0	0	0	0	0	0	0	0	0	0	0	0	0	0	0	0	0	0	0	0	0	0	22	13	40	24	
Dominance—one-upmanship, superiority, competition (28)	0	0	0	0	0	0	0	0	0	0	0	0	0	0	0	0	0	0	0	0	0	0	0	0	0	0	0	0	0	0	0	0	0	0	13	33	17	
Historical import—event's identification with stream of humanity (2)	0	0	0	0	0	0	0	0	0	0	0	0	0	0	0	0	0	0	0	0	0	0	0	0	0	0	0	0	0	0	0	0	0	0	0	22	6	
Status—prestige, position, external image (31)	0	0	0	0	0	0	0	0	0	0	0	0	0	0	0	0	0	0	0	0	0	0	0	0	0	0	0	0	0	0	0	0	0	0	0	0	15	
Sexual fulfillment—sex life or love life (3)	0	0	0	0	0	0	0	0	0	0	0	0	0	0	0	0	0	0	0	0	0	0	0	0	0	0	0	0	0	0	0	0	0	0	0	0	0	

NOTE: Numbers in parentheses refer to the original sequence used in the matrix questionnaire.

[a] Items were randomized in the questionnaire; this order is after diagonalization of the responses.

101

These two characteristics are:

4 – Essentially identical or a part of.
3 – Very similar or very close.
2 – Somewhat similar.
1 – Distantly related.
0 – Not related at all.

Fifteen of the respondents completed the matrix. Their individual responses were aggregated by summing the absolute values of all cells of the fifteen matrices; the summed matrix is presented in table 4-1. A matrix diagonalization routine was used to isolate subclusters within the thirty-eight general characteristics.[13] The results of the initial diagonalization were not satisfactory, and a flow graph was drawn (figure 4-5) that shows isolated clusters, using inter-item pair associates that occurred in the upper octile of the group responses. Twelve clusters of characteristics were isolated as supracharacteristics.[e] A list of these twelve supracharacteristics was fed back to the group of respondents on the successive two rounds with instructions:

Please weigh the relative importance of the 12 aggregated characteristics. In the column headed "weight on the attached list, distribute 100 "points" among the 12 groups—i.e., for each characteristic group, write a number between 0 and 100 to indicate relative importance, where the numbers total 100.

The results are shown in table 4-2. As with other feedback responses in this exercise, the median weights changed very little from round to round. There was a moderate convergence of quartiles toward the median on the second round. Intrigued by the lack of change in the second round for this question, the experimenters asked the group in the final meeting how they had answered the weighting question. The majority of respondents reported they had deviated from the initial instruction to answer all questions in the framework of how they thought others felt, and in fact, on this question had answered in terms of what their own weighting would be. Given the individual mental set with which they answered the weighting question, therefore, it is not surprising that there would not be a great convergence in responses.

In the process of analyzing the flow graph, it was obvious that one characteristic (sex) had large interrelationships with most of the other characteristics. This was not checked for in the diagonalization algorithm, a fact responsible for the unsatisfactory aggregation produced by that method.

Time Dynamics of the Quality-of-Life Index

In order to determine the time duration of effects of events, the following was asked on two successive rounds:

[e]Other cluster analysis and multidimensional scaling routines have been applied to the data with results consistent with these twelve clusters of characteristics.

103

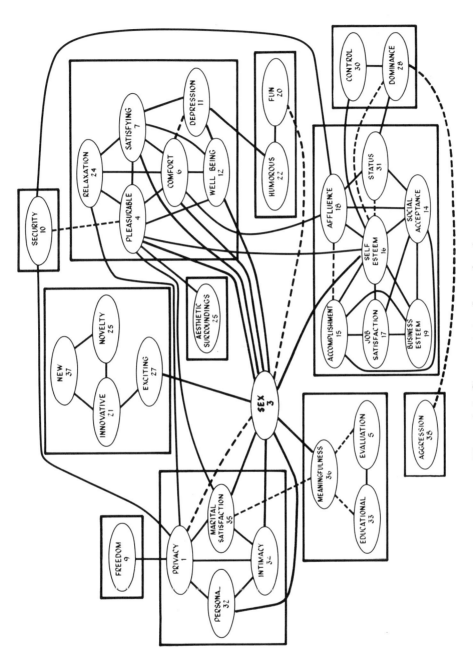

Figure 4-5. Characteristics: Interralatedness.

Table 4-2
Aggregated Characteristic Weights

Characteristic	Description	Relative Weights					
		First Individual Estimate			Second Estimate with Feedback		
		Lower Quartile	Median	Upper Quartile	Lower Quartile	Median	Upper Quartile
A. Aesthetic	(25) Aesthetic surroundings	3	4	10	3	4	7
B. Freedom	(9) Freedom, lack of restraints, lack of compulsion	6	9	15	6	10	14
C. Pleasurable	(4) Pleasurable, satisfying, feeling of contentment, (6) Comfort, (7) Satisfying to the senses, warm, (24) Relaxation, easing, recreation, leisure, rest, (12) Physical well-being, health, feeling good and "alive," (11) Depression, sorrow, grief, tragedy. (negative)	8	10	15	10	10	10
D. Meaningfulness	(5) Evaluative, brings feedback, (33) Educational, (36) Meaningfulness	5	10	12	7	10	12
E. Newness	(21) Innovative, creative, (26) Novelty, surprising, unanticipated, unexpected, (37) New, unfamiliar, (27) Exciting, stimulating, arousing	5	6	10	5	6	9
F. Aggression	(38) Aggression, interpersonal conflict, blowing off steam	0	2	5	0	2	4

G. Sexual fulfillment	(3) Sexual fulfillment—sex life or love life	5	10	13	6	10	13
H. Security	(10) Security, safety, not anxious or threatened	5	9	11	5	10	11
I. Dominance	(28) Dominance, one-upmanship, superiority, competition, (30) Control, directedness, under one's own power	1	4	6	1	4	5
J. Affection	(1) Privacy, withdrawn from soc. vis., (32) Personal, (34) Intimacy, affection, friendship, closeness, tenderness, (35) Marital satisfaction	7	10	18	9	11	15
K. Fun	(22) Humorous, (20) Playfulness, fun	2	5	8	3	5	6
L. Status	(14) Social acceptance, belonging, recognition by peer group, (15) Accomplishment, achievement, meeting goals, success, (16) Self-esteem, ego satisfaction, pride, self-image, (17) Job satisfaction, job motivation, enjoyment of work, (19) Business esteem, job progress, success in work, (18) Material well-being, affluence, material comforts, (31) Status, prestige, position, external image	5	12	20	6	14	15

Note: Numbers in parentheses refer to items on the characteristic list used in the Delphi questionnaire.

Historical Events

For those individuals who make evaluations, what is the effective span of time in the past that influences the evaluation? (Assume a "normal," noncrisis period.) Express your answer in whatever units seem most appropriate.

First Round Response (in days)			Second Round Response (in days)		
Lower Quartile	Median	Upper Quartile	Lower Quartile	Median	Upper Quartile
6 1/2	45	180	25	45	75

Anticipated Events

In general (for a "normal," noncrisis period), how far into the future does the average individual project his expectations (i.e., what is the individual's time horizon). For this question, please give a numerical estimate.

First Round Response (in days)			Second Round Response (in days)		
Lower Quartile	Median	Upper Quartile	Lower Quartile	Median	Upper Quartile
105	365	821	202	365	365

There was clearly a convergence shown in these questions while the median time-span remained constant. The second time the time-span question was asked, the respondents were also asked for "typical" events of the type they were thinking about. Results indicated three major classes of events for both the future and past horizon. These were, in terms of number of times cited, as follows:

	Past	Future
Job-related events		
Loss of job	3	4
Promotion	7	5
Failure of expected results to occur	1	—
Vacation	2	7
Moving to new home	2	6

Other Past Events

Accident, death, divorce, sickness, car trouble, receiving test results, personal encounter, dropping out of society, major purchase.

Other Future Events

Social events, being drafted, expecting a hot date, graduation, achievement, having a baby.

It should also be noted that future events had a much longer time horizon than past events. Other research supports a conclusion that the time horizon for past and future events is determined by personal characteristics.[14]

The respondents in the second round were also asked to compare the relative impact of the past event with the same event if it had happened only a day ago (yesterday) and to express the answer as a ratio of the present impact if the event had occurred yesterday to the present impact of the event if it had occurred at the past horizon. A similar question was also asked concerning the future event. At the median horizon for both past and future events (45 days and 365 days, respectively), the median relative impact reported was 5 to 1.

In order to pursue the role of expectations, the following question was asked on the third and fourth rounds:

Roughly speaking, two kinds of events appear to influence the quality of life of an individual, relatively long-term events (moving, vacations, job changes) and relatively short-term (social events, typical job-connected events, family life). Please estimate the relative importance for an individual's quality of life of unusual, long-term events (anticipated or remembered) as compared with short-term, more typical events. The comparative role of these two kinds of events may differ among individuals. Indicate the possible range over individuals by giving the proportionate effect for an "average individual," and for two extreme individuals—one more highly influenced by long-term events, and one less highly influenced.

Relative portion (0 to 100) of an individual's self-evaluation determined by long-term events:

a. For an "average" individual

Third Round			Fourth Round Reevaluation		
Lower Quartile	Median	Upper Quartile	Lower Quartile	Median	Upper Quartile
26	40	50	30	40	50

b. For an individual highly influenced

Third Round			Fourth Round Reevaluation		
Lower Quartile	Median	Upper Quartile	Lower Quartile	Median	Upper Quartile
50	70	80	55	70	75

c. For an individual less highly influenced by long-term events

Third Round			Fourth Round Reevaluation		
Lower Quartile	Median	Upper Quartile	Lower Quartile	Median	Upper Quartile
6	20	30	12	20	22

Thus, again, the medians did not change and there was convergence of quartiles toward the medians.

Other Properties of the Quality-of-Life Index

Other factors were investigated briefly in this exercise. First, there was a very high concurrence in the belief that those more highly educated are likely to make explicit evaluations more often than those less highly educated.

Are those more highly educated more likely to make explicit evaluations than those less highly educated? (Check one of the three options below):

a. The higher the educational level, the more explicit the evaluation, or   16
b. Educational level makes no difference, or   7
c. The lower the educational level, the more explicit the evaluation   1

However, while anticipation of the future does not depend on the level of education, it does have a role in the QOL of an individual.

How extensive a role does anticipation of the future play in the overall evaluation? (Check those statements with which you concur):

a. In general, anticipation plays a major role in the individual's running score.   11
b. The effect of anticipation varies widely with the individual.   14
c. The magnitude of the effect of anticipation increases with the individual's level of education.   5
d. The effect of anticipation varies greatly with the events anticipated.   12

There was also a high concurrence with respect to belief that the running score or QOL index involves a comparison level composed of a set of ideals or objectives, as is seen in the response to the following question.

Does the running score involve a comparison level (i.e., a standard or set of standards in terms of which the score is measured—sometimes referred to as aspiration level)?

a. Yes, or   20
b. No   4
If yes, then
a. Is this comparison level primarily composed of a set of "ideals," i.e., a standard against which the individual's current condition or life situation is compared, or   12
b. Is this comparison level primarily the level that divides a satisfactory life from an unsatisfactory one, or   6
c. Other?   2

However, the QOL indexes do not include all elements of an individual's life, as each person tends to omit important segments of his life experience from his evaluation of his life.

Does the running score tend to include all the elements that are directly involved in the individual's life? (Check one):

a. The running score includes all elements, or   4
b. There are usually important segments left out, depending on the individual's situation or recent experiences, or   16
c. There are elements that are left out generally by all persons.   4

Finally, a majority of the respondents agreed that the QOL index is an expression of how things are going rather than a guide for future action for most people.

To what extent is the score a motive for action or a guide for planning?

a. The score is mainly an overall assessment, expressing "how things are going."   18
b. The score acts primarily as an indicator of "where to go," i.e., as a motive and guide for action.   5

Preliminary Application in Two Individual Decision-Making Contexts

The primary purpose of this section is to report on an exercise in which the set of QOL characteristics elicited in the study reviewed in the previous section was used by a small group of mid-career federal executives to evaluate some alternative courses of action in two decision-making situations. In addition, there is a discussion of possible future studies and applications of QOL findings.

It is premature to recommend serious application of the available QOL measurement tools in major decision-making, particularly at the governmental level. Far more definitional work, structuring of the methodology and testing will be needed before taking that step. On the other hand, it is instructive to experiment with the tools even in their current, relatively crude state, for selected individual decisions. The results of some experiments of this kind are documented in this section.

The participants were thirteen mid-career federal executives who were on a one-year leave of absence from their agencies to study systems analysis at the University of California at Irvine (UCI). Seven members of this group had already participated in the earlier QOL exercise described in the preceding section. The other six respondents had not participated in that exercise and were only vaguely familiar with the QOL concepts and methodology with which we had been working.

The questionnaire presented to the group involved two sets of decision alternatives. In one case, they were asked to evaluate eight different career/life environments, each of which was described in about one paragraph. In the second case, they were asked to evaluate five different modes of transportation for commuting between the UCI campus and The Rand Corporation, a round-trip distance of 110 miles. At the time, the participants were making this trip twice a week by car pool. The questionnaire, including the one-paragraph descriptions of environments and travel modes, is reproduced as appendix B.

The evaluation was to be made against each of the twelve QOL characteristics developed during the earlier exercise. The respondents were asked to give a zero rating to a characteristic for a particular environment or transportation mode if it merely provided an acceptable level for that characteristic. If an environment or mode offered an attractively superior amount or degree of a particular characteristic, they were asked to give it a positive rating on a scale between 0 and 10. If, on the other hand, an environment or mode provided a detractive or inferior aspect with regard to a particular characteristic, the respondents were to rate the value they placed upon that disadvantage on a negative scale between 0 and -10.

In addition to the evaluation process, the participants were asked to rank each of the environments and each of the modes in order of personal preference. The basic test was to compare the expressed order of personal preference with an order of desirability derived from a numerical factor based upon the respondent's rating of the characteristics for each alternative. For the latter process, we required weights of relative importance which each respondent placed upon each of the characteristics. As mentioned previously, these were obtained during the earlier exercise by asking each respondent to distribute 100 points over the twelve characteristics. For those seven respondents who had participated in the prior effort, individual weights were already on hand. From the six new respondents, weights were solicited.

Using an individual's ratings of the QOL characteristics in each environment and mode, and the individual's personal set of weights, the following formula was applied to determine a computed "desirability factor" for each environment and each transportation mode:

$$\text{Worth of job } j = \sum_{i=1}^{12} \text{(Weight given to characteristic } i) \times \text{(Rating of characteristic } i \text{ for job } j).$$

After applying this operation to all modes and all environments, the modes and environments were placed in numerical order according to their aggregated desirability factors. This provided a new, computed order of preference for each individual, ostensibly based upon how the respondent should have ranked his preference had his choices been entirely consistent with the weights he gave to the characteristics and the ratings he gave those characteristics with respect to the various modes and environments.

The QOL of Eight Idealized Environments

Table 4-3 shows the actual indicated preference rankings and the computed preference rankings by the number of individuals who selected each environment for each choice, first through eighth. The outstanding comparative aspect of table 4-3 is that the group's indicated choices as a whole were not substantially different from those derived from a quantitative evaluation of the ratings. Only the sixth and seventh place environment changed order in overall preference, and this is nonsignificant. It is inferred that the individual order of selection was based upon a reasonably rational and consistent evaluation process, and that the QOL rating scheme represents a fairly reasonable approximation of that process. There was, however, some considerable shifting in the particular rankings for each environment.

The comparisons of indicated versus computed rankings of environments, by individual respondent, are shown in table 4-4. This table shows that, on the whole, correlation coefficients between the two sets of rankings were fairly high. The correlations ranged from 0.50 to 0.95, with a median at 0.83. Interestingly enough, the correlations for those who had not participated in the earlier exercise, and thus were less familiar with the concepts with which we were working, were just as good as those for respondents who had participated in the earlier exercise.

In an effort to determine the validity of the process for establishing a satisfactory group weight, we also applied our weight-rating formula using previously generated group weights (median values) for each of the characteristics instead of the respondent's own individual set of weights. The results of this computation are shown in table 4-4. We were encouraged to find that, although the range of correlations increased (from a low of 0.42 to a high of 0.97), the median went up to 0.88. Given the obvious limitations of such a small and fairly homogeneous sample, this still gives some support to the probable validity of broader applications of sample sociometric factors derived through such a process.

Another interesting facet of the data contained in table 4-4 is the fact that nearly every respondent selected one environment in a significantly different order from the computation. There are, of course, several possible explanations for such differences. One is that there is some characteristic or criterion that respondents used to evaluate the environments that is not included among our list of twelve. (The high correlation in the majority of cases argues against such a possibility, but does not rule it out.) A second possibility is that a respondent

Table 4-3
Group Ranking of Environments

Idealized Environments	Preference Rankings								Average Group Indexes
	1st	2d	3d	4th	5th	6th	7th	8th	
Dartmouth College									
Public Admin. Program									
Indicated Choice	7	4	2	—	—	—	—	—	1.62
Computed choice	10	3	—	—	—	—	—	—	1.2
Virgin Islands									
Program Planning									
Indicated choice	3	5	2	2	—	—	1	—	2.62
Computed choice	2	7	1	1	—	—	2	—	2.8
Own Agency									
Indicated choice	1	1	5	1	—	3	1	1	4.23
Computed choice	—	1	5	1	2	2	1	1	4.5
Wheeling									
Asst. to City Manager									
Indicated choice	1	1	—	3	5	1	3	—	5.08
Computed choice	—	1	1	6	2	—	2	1	4.7
Cleveland									
Asst. to Mayor									
Indicated choice	—	—	1	3	3	3	2	1	5.38
Computed choice	—	—	3	2	1	4	2	1	5.2
Aerospace									
Systems Analyst									
Indicated choice	1	1	—	—	3	4	2	2	5.55
Computed choice	—	1	—	2	3	2	3	2	5.7
Small Instrument Lab									
Asst. Vice President									
Indicated choice	—	1	3	1	1	—	3	4	5.62
Computed choice	—	—	2	1	4	2	2	2	5.5
Saigon									
AID Program Analyst									
Indicated choice	1	—	—	3	1	2	1	5	5.92
Computed choice	1	—	1	—	1	3	1	6	6.3

might consciously rank a job highly even though he knows he will not enjoy it very much because he believes it would lead to an even better opportunity later in his career.

One is immediately struck by the fact that there was a strikingly high group consensus on the Dartmouth job. This comes from a group of individuals with

Table 4-4
Individual Rankings of Environments

Individual Respondents		1st	2d	3d	4th	5th	6th	7th	8th	Correlation
					Rank of Choice of Environment					
1.	Individual's choice	D	O	I	L	A	W	C	V	
	Computed order (personal weights)	D	O	I	W	L	C	A	V	.88
	Computed order (Delphi weights)	D	O	I	L	W	A	C	V	.97
2.	Individual's choice	D	I	O	W	A	V	C	L	
	Computed order (personal weights)	D	I	O	A	V	C	W	L	.86
	Computed order (Delphi weights)	D	I	O	A	V	C	W	L	.86
3.	Individual's choice	D	W	I	C	V	A	L	O	
	Computed order (personal weights)	D	W	O	I	A	V	C	L	.55
	Computed order (Delphi weights)	D	W	O	I	A	V	C	L	.55
4.[a]	Individual's choice	I	D	O	V	A	C	W	L	
	Computed order (personal weights)	D	I	O	W	L	C	A	V	.52
	Computed order (Delphi weights)	D	I	O	W	L	C	A	V	.52
5.	Individual's choice	I	L	D	C	W	A	O	V	
	Computed order (personal weights)	D	I	W	C	A	O	L	V	.57
	Computed order (Delphi weights)	D	I	W	O	A	C	L	V	.42
6.	Individual's choice	D	I	L	C	V	O	W	A	
	Computed order (personal weights)	D	I	V	C	W	O	L	A	.71
	Computed order (Delphi weights)	D	I	V	C	W	O	A	L	.59
7.	Individual's choice	O	I	D	W	L	C	A	V	
	Computed order (personal weights)	I	D	O	W	L	A	C	V	.90
	Computed order (Delphi weights)	I	O	D	L	W	C	A	V	.95
8.	Individual's choice	D	A	I	C	W	O	V	L	
	Computed order (personal weights)	D	I	L	A	C	V	O	W	.50
	Computed order (Delphi weights)	D	I	A	C	O	W	L	V	.92
9.[a]	Individual's choice	A	D	L	O	W	C	I	V	
	Computed order (personal weights)	D	A	L	W	O	C	I	V	.95
	Computed order (Delphi weights)	D	A	L	W	O	C	I	V	.95
10.[a]	Individual's choice	V	D	C	I	W	A	L	O	
	Computed order (personal weights)	V	D	C	W	A	L	I	O	.86
	Computed order (Delphi weights)	D	V	I	C	W	L	A	O	.92
11.[a]	Individual's choice	I	D	L	V	A	O	W	C	
	Computed order (personal weights)	I	D	O	L	W	A	V	C	.71
	Computed order (Delphi weights)	I	D	L	A	W	V	O	C	.88
12.[a]	Individual's choice	D	I	O	W	C	A	L	V	
	Computed order (personal weights)	D	I	C	W	O	L	A	V	.86
	Computed order (Delphi weights)	D	I	W	C	O	L	A	V	.90
13.[a]	Individual's choice	D	I	O	V	C	W	L	A	
	Computed order (personal weights)	D	I	C	O	L	V	W	A	.83
	Computed order (Delphi weights)	D	I	L	C	O	W	V	A	.64

NOTE: Letters represent environments: D = Dartmouth; I = Virgin Islands; O - Own Job; W = Wheeling; C = Cleveland; A = Aerospace; L = Small Instrument Lab; and V = Saigon.
[a]Respondents who did not participate in earlier exercise.

no background of teaching and fairly strong commitments to careers in the federal government. Six of the participants were raised in urban areas (greater than 100,000 population), and seven were from strictly rural areas. In an attempt to explain this and other group response patterns, we turned to a detailed analysis of the ratings the group gave each environment for each QOL characteristic.

Figure 4-6 shows the aggregate ratings given each of the characteristics for each of the eight environments. It is clear that the Dartmouth assignment was the only one, in the group's view, that provided better than satisfactory levels for all twelve QOL characteristics. Each of the other environments received one or more negative characteristic ratings from the group as a whole. For the Saigon assignment, the group's least desired choice, eight of the twelve characteristics fell below the satisfactory level. The number below each environment heading is an aggregate desirability factor, derived by summing the results of multiplying the aggregate rating for each characteristic times the weight for the characteristic, and dividing by thirteen (the number of respondents).

As Figure 4-6 shows, the respondents rated all the environments fairly high on meaningfulness, status, and newness. This is not unreasonable considering the specific nature of the environments. (These are described in detail in appendix B.) It should be pointed out that all the career/living environments offered the respondents reasonably significant increases in salary. In addition, all the positions, with the possible exception of the aerospace job, promised fairly clear increases in stature and responsibility for most of the respondents. Obviously, any departure from their present job/living environment would have some element of newness in it. Thus, the rather high overall ratings for status, newness, and meaningfulness were not unpredictable. Indeed, most of the characteristic ratings appear to be fairly logical when viewed a posteriori, although it would have been difficult to have predicted the overall ordering of desirability.

It is worth noting that the data displayed on the chart imply the existence of a fairly intricate tradeoff process. The measures are so crude, however, and the sample size so small, that it is really impossible to develop any specific hypotheses. Still, a chart like this one, with these findings, could conceivably provide a very useful analytical tool, for example, to a company recruiter. From the chart, it is clear that the handsome salary offered by the aerospace company is an insufficient inducement to make that job as attractive as six of the other alternatives, which offered substantially lower salaries.

What actions might the aerospace company take to correct this situation, based on the data shown in figure 4-6? The aerospace company's weakest point is the characteristic designated freedom. Thus, might not they consider reducing their salary offer and compensate for this weakness by offering a six-month sabbatical to its systems analysts every three years? They also were rated poorly on the characteristic of meaningfulness. Might not an offer of research

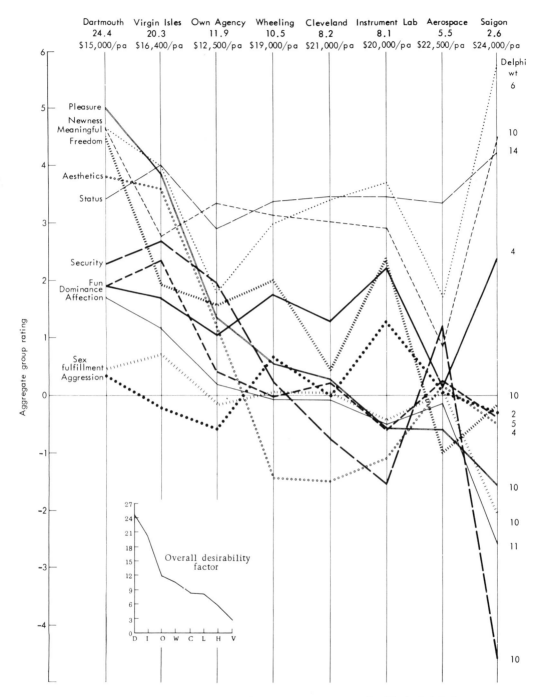

Figure 4-6. Aggregate Group Characteristic Ratings for Each Job-Life Environment.

115

time and facilities or a staff publishing program increase the respondent's rating of this characteristic?

Similar rough analyses can be made for each of the other environments. In this respect, this particular QOL rating scheme has some practical applications that can be tested. However, it should be pointed out that we are working with an evaluation of desirability. It is by no means clear that the respondents would actually choose the environment they rated first if they were really faced with the choice. And this very point brings us back again to the question of what affects the level of an individual's QOL.

If our list of characteristics is complete, and the respondents' ratings of the characteristics are accurate (for each individual), then we would have defined, in theory, the order of environments in which the individual would be happiest, second happiest, third happiest, etc. If the individual were completely rational, we would assume he would actually select the environment that would make him happiest. We know, however, that people often act illogically, and indeed, often act in ways that do not suit their best interests.

These irrationalities are sometimes conscious, sometimes not. They are sometimes freely arrived at, sometimes forced. Returning to our environments, a number of examples might be given. For instance, consider the case of a man who is deep in debt, who would feel constrained to take a position with a high cash salary, such as the Cleveland job, even though he would much prefer the Virgin Islands. Consider a man who selects the aerospace job so his wife can be close to her elderly parents, even though he personally would have preferred the Dartmouth job.

One might reasonably argue that the individual will really have made the optimal decision for himself in this situation, having made a tradeoff, in which he has exchanged some measure of his personal happiness for a comparable value in the form of domestic tranquility and a sense of well-being on the part of his wife. On the other hand, he has, perhaps, adopted a minimax strategy, or he may simply have acquiesced to his wife's emphatic demands; but whatever his immediate motivation, it cannot actually be called a tradeoff or compromise, but rather a capitulation in a confrontation between two absolutes. In the case in point, there is no realistic halfway measure between the two alternatives. That is, the husband could not realistically work in Dartmouth while living with his wife in Los Angeles. Similarly, there could be no job/living environment that combined some features of the two alternatives, because they represent separate, unique entities not subject to compromise. Thus, a decision to take the aerospace job because, in essence, it was perceived to be the only way to preserve the marriage, does not necessarily make the decision optimal, merely expedient. Dartmouth will probably still be the more desirable job/living environment in the man's eyes, even though he opts for Los Angeles.

Barriers to optimization may be internal as well as external, as in the case of a man who is terribly unsure of his own capabilities. He is not very likely to pick any alternative that appears to offer greater responsibility or authority than he currently holds, even though he might find several of the alternatives more desirable than his own. Similarly, the so-called Puritan ethic might well dissuade an individual from selecting the Virgin Islands job, even though he found the job otherwise most appealing.

To the extent that these and other such barriers come between an individual and his desires, he is likely to make decisions that may be less than optimal in terms of the quality of his life, or his happiness, or his sense of well-being. In the parlance of today's young people, these limitations and constraints might be termed "hang-ups." It is not unlikely that such hang-ups account for at least some of the inconsistencies between the indicated and computed preferences for the alternatives in this exercise.

It is widely accepted that all individuals possess variable and complex value systems for making judgments and decisions. Values may be viewed as falling into two broad categories: (1) normative values, derived through enculturation processes and usually acquired during childhood and adolescence, and (2) functional values (or role values), which are attached to the various roles an individual fills throughout his life. In this context, values may be said to represent the decision criteria an individual will use in attempting to secure an optimal mix of QOL characteristics.

Figure 4-7 shows a theoretical interaction between values and QOL characteristics. Because people undergo enculturation from the outset of their existence, normative values will tend to be dominant early in an individual's life. In fact,

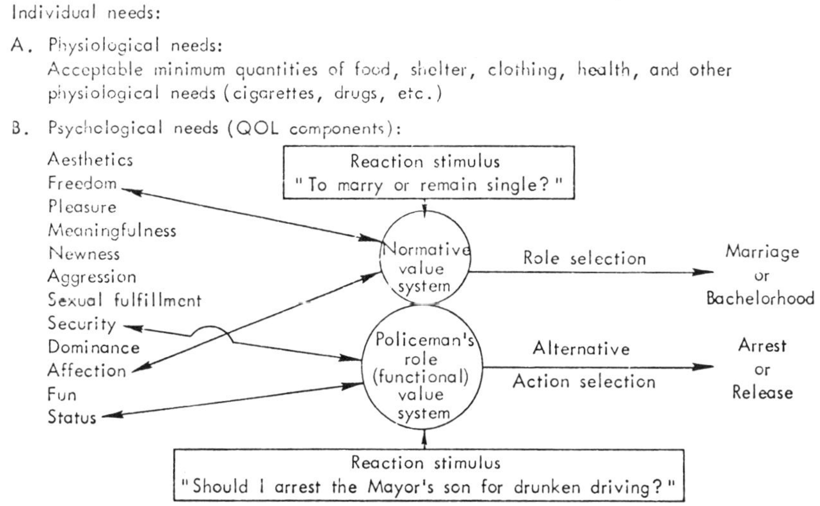

Figure 4-7. Theoretical Interaction between Values and QOL Characteristics.

they will be instrumental in determining many of the roles that an individual selects. As an individual abandons the dependent or child role, he will begin a process of acquiring additional roles. Figure 4-7 is a highly simplified model of what is, in reality, a very complex interactive relationship.

In each of the two examples shown, the individual is faced with a decision (reaction stimulus). In one case, the individual must decide whether or not to marry. If he has a high need (weight) on the QOL component affection, and his normative value system indicates marriage as the optimal way to assure satisfaction of that need, the individual will doubtless take the plunge. If, on the other hand, the individual feels a strong need for freedom or dominance, his value system may tell him that marriage will not provide an adequate level of satisfaction for these needs and he will remain single. Or, he may feel a strong need for affection, but an unhappy childhood experience with hostile or divorced parents may lead to a normative value system that puts little utility upon marriage as a satisfier of his needs for affection.

In the case of the policeman, his functional value system in his role as policeman will tell him that arresting the mayor's son will threaten to remove some degree of security, though it will enhance his self-esteem (a component of the QOL characteristic, status, shown in table 4-2). His decision may be further complicated by other roles he may fill, and the functional values in those roles will indicate significant benefits for maintaining the family's security and severe penalties for jeopardizing the family's security. Thus, in the face of this interactive process, the policeman must make his decision. If his need for self-esteem is great, he may act in direct opposition to the police officer and household head value systems and arrest the miscreant.

In this context, a sophisticated industrial society might be compared to a maturing, prospering middleaged man. As his horizons become broader, his tastes become more cosmopolitan, and his capacities to indulge his desires increase, he is faced with an ever-increasing number of restrictions and constraints, which are products of his stature in society, his professional role, his family status, and the patterns of habit and expectation that the interrelationships of these functions impose upon him. To the extent that our modern American industrial society presents us simultaneously with greater mobility and broader horizons for perceived alternative courses of action and with greater and more numerous hang-ups, we will naturally face greater barriers to optimizing the quality of our lives. Moreover, our actual sense of well-being or self-assessment of happiness may well be related to the degree to which we are conscious of the existence and effects of these hang-ups on our lives.

The QOL and Several Modes of Transportation

For the respondents, and indeed for most of us, a choice among several methods of commuting to work is a very real decision, but one which would presumably involve a relatively unsophisticated set of decision variables. Still, in order to test the practical applicability of our QOL characteristics, we asked the respondents to evaluate five alternative modes of transportation using all twelve of the characteristics. (Detailed descriptions of the five alternative modes are in appendix B.) The choice among five alternative modes of commutation between the UCI campus area and Rand represented potential solutions to a real problem facing the respondents, who made the trip, by car pool, twice each week.

Table 4-5 is similar to table 4-3 and shows how respondents ranked the desirability of the five transportation modes. The computed rankings of the modes based on evaluation of each of the QOL characteristics are shown.

Here there were not only changes within the ranking of choices for each mode, but there was a significant change in the overall order of ranking for group choice. As might be supposed, the individual correlations were not nearly as good as they were for the environments. The range of individual correlations was from −0.20 to 0.90, with the median falling at 0.70. Use of the detailed characteristic weights in lieu of the overall rankings in this case made no significant differences in the order or in the correlation coefficients.

Table 4-6 shows the individually expressed order of preference in comparison with the computed order of preference for the five modes, along with the individual correlations. Unlike the individual ratings of environments, we were able to identify an almost consistently misrated item—the train. The train almost

Table 4-5
Overall Rankings of Transportation Modes

Transportation Mode	Preference Rankings					Average Group Indexes
	1st	2d	3d	4th	5th	
Hovercraft						
Indicated choice	7	6	−	−	−	1.46
Computed choice	8	2	3	−	−	1.62
Aircraft						
Indicated choice	3	7	2	1	−	2.08
Computed choice	1	7	2	2	1	2.62
Car Pool						
Indicated choice	2	−	4	5	2	3.38
Computed choice	2	1	−	1	9	4.08
Limousine						
Indicated choice	1	−	6	4	2	3.46
Computed choice	1	2	2	6	2	3.46
Train						
Indicated choice	−	−	1	3	9	4.62
Computed choice	−	2	6	3	2	3.38

Table 4-6

Indicated and Computed Preferences for Modes of Transportation, with Correlation Coefficients

Individual Respondent	Rank of Mode Choice					Correlation Coefficient
	1st	2d	3d	4th	5th	
1. Indicated choice	P	H	L	A	T	
Computed choice	L	H	T	A	P	−.20
2. Indicated choice	L	H	A	P	T	
Computed choice	L	P	H	A	T	.70
3. Indicated choice	A	H	L	T	P	
Computed choice	H	A	T	L	P	.80
4.[a] Indicated choice	H	A	P	L	T	
Computed choice	H	A	T	L	P	.60
5. Indicated choice	H	A	P	L	T	
Computed choice	H	A	L	T	P	.70
6. Indicated choice	H	A	P	T	L	
Computed choice	H	A	T	P	L	.90
7. Indicated choice	H	A	L	P	T	
Computed choice	H	T	A	L	P	.40
8. Indicated choice	A	H	T	P	L	
Computed choice	P	A	H	L	T	.20
9.[a] Indicated choice	P	H	A	L	T	
Computed choice	P	L	H	T	A	.40
10.[a] Indicated choice	H	A	L	T	P	
Computed choice	H	A	T	L	P	.90
11.[a] Indicated choice	H	A	L	P	T	
Computed choice	A	H	L	T	P	.80
12.[a] Indicated choice	A	H	L	P	T	
Computed choice	A/H[b]	H/A	T	L	P	.70
13.[a] Indicated choice	H	A	P	L	T	
Computed choice	H	T	A	L	P	.30

Note: L = Limousine, H = Hovercraft, A = Aircraft, P = Present Method (Car Pool), T = Train.

[a]Respondents who did not participate in earlier exercise.

[b]Computed ratings show equal preference for Hovercraft and aircraft. Therefore, correlation coefficient is approximated.

always fell low as an expressed preference, but its QOL weight computation placed it as a strong third in the overall group preference.

Several individuals wrote comments on their responses that helped us to identify the problem here. It was fairly clear that most people felt the train was, in the abstract, a fairly appealing mode of travel. This appears to have been the manner in which they rated the train as a transportation mode. However, in making a choice for the practical personal decision posed by the questionnaire, most people rated it last because of: (1) its disadvantageous time schedule, and/or (2) the inconvenience of access for the specific trip (i.e., commute to station, train to downtown L.A., cab to Santa Monica, etc.). It should also be noted that some people said that they ranked the modes not according to personal preference, but according to personal preference plus a realistic possibility of the mode's actual adoption. In such cases, the respondents ranked the Hovercraft and the aircraft low, even though they gave these modes high QOL ratings, because they felt they were too costly to be realistically considered for adoption. Here, clearly, we are dealing with some hang-ups, some artificial barriers to the individual's free choice of a course of action that would be optimal for his QOL characteristics.

Along that line, we asked a question that evoked some interesting responses. For each of the transportation modes, it was initially assumed that all costs would be borne by the Public Policy Research Organization, the institution under whose aegis the respondents were studying at UCI. In the questionnaire, after asking the respondents to rate and rank the transportation modes, we pointed out the high cost of the Hovercraft and aircraft as being a probable barrier to their adoption. We then asked the respondents to indicate how much they would be willing to pay out of their own pockets each day to subsidize each of the two expensive travel modes. The responses indicated a span of $0/per day to $5/per day for Hovercraft, with a median response of $3.50. The average of the responses was $2.84. For aircraft, the spread of responses was the same, $0 to $5 per day, but the median was $2.50, with an average of $2.36.

When these responses are combined, as in figure 4-8, we can begin to see, once again, some sort of tradeoff relationship, although one can only speculate as to what is being traded. Figure 4-8 shows, in the same manner as figure 4-6, the aggregate ratings given by the group to each QOL characteristic for each mode of transportation. There are some very sharp differences between the overall pattern of characteristic ratings for the transportation modes and that for the environments.

For example, only one characteristic diminishes continually across all eight of the environments—pleasure. Six characteristics diminish directly in order of computed preference for the transportation modes, however. These are newness, pleasure, aesthetics, fun, status, and meaningfulness. As a result, the overall desirability factor for the modes produces a more steeply declining monotonic curve than that for the environments. In part, of course, this would be expected, since the considerations involved in evaluating the modes are much less complex than those related to the environments. The modes are also more distinctly different from one another than are the environments.

Two particular aspects of figure 4-8 are especially noteworthy. One is the ratings given for security. Even though the descriptions of the modes specifically

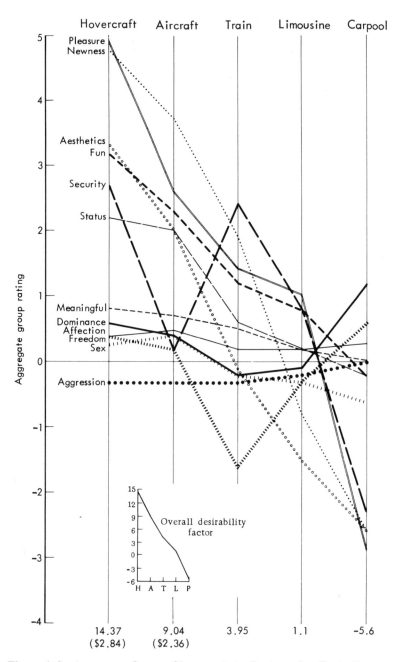

Figure 4–8. Aggregate Group Characteristic Ratings for Each Transportation Mode.

showed the safety rate for the aircraft to be the highest of all the alternatives, the group as a whole felt very insecure about flying. The second prominent specific feature of the graph is the startlingly low rating for freedom that the group gave to the train. Presumably, this is, at least in part, a representation of their dissatisfaction with the inconvenience and complexity of the arrangements associated with the train mode, and the inflexibility of its schedule.

Another striking aspect of figure 4-8 is the very poor rating the group gave the present car pooling arrangement. The aggregate desirability factor for that mode has a negative net value, which would indicate that the group, as a whole, found the arrangement unsatisfactory. Ultimately, one might reason that this particular activity had a detrimental effect on the overall quality of the participants' lives while they were in California. Yet the expressed group preference in table 4-5 showed the respondents ranked car pooling in third place. This would indicate, once again, an interposition of external constraints between the individual and his drive to optimize the quality of his life.

Given the preceding findings, let us consider the probable outcome of our inquiry had the respondents been offered a choice among only three alternative modes: rail, limousine, and car pool. Presumably, according to the indicated preferences in table 4-5, the group's decision would be to rank the order of preference as car pool, limousine, and train, even though their computed preferences indicate that they found the three modes desirable in exactly the opposite order. How might we explain, in some specific way, this apparently illogical behavior?

If we examine the comparative characteristic ratings for the three modes (figure 4-8), it does appear that there are some identifiable tradeoffs. For example, let us consider the relationship between the ratings for the train and the car pool. First of all, let us eliminate from consideration those characteristics that received relatively similar ratings for both the modes in question. These characteristics would be aggression, sex, affection, meaningfulness, and status. This leaves us with the following strong and weak points for the two modes in question (median ratings times group weights):

	Train			Car Pool	
Strong:	Security	+24		Freedom	+6
	Newness	+19		Dominance	+4.8
	Pleasure	+14			10.8
	Fun	+ 6			
	Aesthetics	− 0.4			
		62.6			
Weak:	Freedom	−16		Security	−23
	Dominance	− 1.2		Newness	−15.6
		−17.2		Pleasure	−29

		Fun	— 1
		Aesthetics	−10.4
			−79
Net:		+45.5	−68.2

Were it not for the weighting system, it might perhaps be possible to say that the respondents would be willing to trade away the advantages offered by the train for the advantages of the car pool. However, when we multiply the group's aggregate rates times the Delphi rates, we see that there is clearly not a tradeoff equilibrium between the two modes overall. However, it should be pointed out that the respondents receive $12.10 for each day that they drive. Thus, they are being compensated, in some measure, for the disadvantages of driving. This represents, on a rotational driver basis, $24.20 per month per participant.

It seems hard to believe that the respondents would be willing to select the car pool over the train on the basis of this modest stipend. Another obvious possibility is that the weights are wrong. Well, certainly no claim can be made that the weights are absolutely correct, but, on the other hand, their overall performance for us in this exercise would indicate that they are fairly sound approximations of the group's value system with respect to the characteristics.

At the risk of being accused of copping-out, we would suggest another explanation. As mentioned above, it appears that the group evaluated the rail mode in the abstract, rather than as it actually existed in this decision situation. Moreover, it would appear that most of the respondents did not include consideration of the taxicab leg of the rail mode in their characteristic ratings. Indeed, although the respondents were asked to evaluate the five alternative commuting schemes, it is more likely that their ratings were largely representative of their feelings about the five alternative primary modes of travel. (This, in large part, may have been a fault of the wording of the questionnaire itself.)

In addition, their choices probably reflect a much broader spectrum of considerations than the modes themselves. One such consideration might have been the reimbursement. Another might have been the effect of arriving home at 9 P.M. as opposed to arriving at 6 P.M. or 7 P.M. What utility might the respondents have had for these hours? What would have been the effect upon the family life? How badly did the respondents need that time for studying? How useful for study was the time between the close of business at Rand at 5 P.M. and the departure time of the train at 7 P.M.?

It is difficult to say how many of these considerations went into the expressed preferences, but probably more than were included in the rating system. And perhaps we could legitimately call many of these considerations hang-ups: constraints and barriers to the free action that would be optimal in the eyes of the respondents. There is every reason for us to believe that, if the train had had a more convenient schedule, or if its downtown terminus were as close to Rand as the Santa Monica Pier, it would have fared much better in the group's expressed preferences. Similarly, one might consider the reimbursement a constraint. All of these are mitigating factors that force a logical decision by the respondents to make what is, from the standpoint of the QOL characteristics, an illogical choice.

Now, it may be argued that this single suboptimal decision will contribute to a greater degree of optimization in the decision maker's overall QOL. Indeed, this is probably the case. When viewed in this light, the tradeoffs involved would not all be contained in the data in figure 4-8, but rather some of the utilities would be found, perhaps, in a series of similar charts showing all the uses to which an individual might put the hours of the day. Still, if a particular living environment forces the individual into too many such suboptimal situations, the environment is likely to produce a low QOL level for its inhabitants.

Along this line, and tangential to the commutation decision, it is worthwhile to inject into this discussion the case of a group of salaried professionals in San Clemente, California. These individuals, about twenty of them, work for a small educational film-making concern, which moved from a large city in the Midwest to locate in San Clemente about eighteen months ago. Shortly after the staff members, all of whom had to relocate to the West Coast, had purchased homes and settled down in San Clemente, the firm announced that it was relocating its activities to Hollywood.

Most of the employees could not afford to sell and relocate again so soon. Thus, they were faced with a 175-mile, 4-hour-per-day commutation. After trying this in car pools for a brief time, a number of them concluded that the experience was too exhausting and frustrating to be endured. They decided their only viable alternative was to rent rooms or apartments, either singly or in groups, in Hollywood, near their office, and to come home on weekends.

Needless to say, this decision was met at home with a reaction not dissimilar to that given the Russian liberating forces by the Czechs. It would have been interesting to have done a QOL analysis on the factors involved in this decision. However, it is noteworthy that the employees opted for such an extreme solution to their problem after considering only one alternative. They did not look into the possibility of commuting by rail, even though they were living only minutes from a local train stop, and their office was only a short cab ride from Union Station. Nor did it occur to them that, on a group basis, charter air commutation might prove to be distinctly cheaper than renting sleeping quarters in Hollywood.

Thus, one might also say that another barrier or constraint to an individual's optimizing his QOL would be his own resourcefulness, imagination, and initiative. In a modern, complex, industrial society, not only will barriers to achieving a high-level QOL be greater and more numerous, but they may also be more challenging and costly to overcome.

A Brief Glance Back, and Then . . . Where Do We Go From Here?

In one of the earlier Delphi exercises, we asked the respondents whether or not they believed that most adult Americans maintained some sort of running evaluation of their lives. The median group response to that question was that about 85 percent of adult Americans do keep some kind of "running score" on their lives. The set of QOL characteristics developed by the respondents in that exercise might be thought of as the criteria by which a score might be kept. The data from our subsequent inquiry regarding environments and modes of transportation supports the notion that people keep score; and the high correlations between the indicated and computed preferences indicates that the list of characteristics and their associated weights represent a reasonably accurate approximation of the criteria used in the evaluative process at least by this particular group of individuals.

Subsequently, we have inferred some additional factors from the findings, the most significant of which is that there are probably a fairly large number of barriers and constraints that may interpose themselves between an individual and his attempts to take actions he perceives to be optimal in terms of the QOL characteristics. We have further hypothesized that these barriers may be conscious or unconscious in the individual's evaluative and decision-making processes, and that they may be either internally or externally based.

Certainly, all of this has not been proven conclusively by the little work done so far, but we find these hypotheses are highly appealing from the standpoint of both logic and intuition. They certainly can be tested, and, although the amount of work involved would be substantial, the concepts are sound enough to justify such effort. However, before discussing the matter of further fact-finding, let us examine one other matter of importance: the question of variation in the weights and characteristics across societal subgroupings.

To begin with, it is highly probable that QOL criteria vary to some extent over various racial, social, and economic subgroups. Indeed, we would be amazed if subsequent surveys showed they did not. The question at this point is how much do they vary? Do we have to begin with every subgroup to establish a new set of characteristics? We hope not, and along this line would like to propose another hypothesis, which we must admit has largely intuitive appeal and simplicity to recommend it.

We suggest that, if the list of twelve characteristics we have derived from the responses is fairly accurate for the people who created it, then it may be reasonably accurate for the society as a whole. This does not mean that it is complete, or that it is precisely accurate or optimally organized, by any means. There is no doubt but that it can be greatly refined and improved upon. One thesis is simply that, whatever the list of characteristics is, it is valid throughout the society. What will change across various social subgroupings, however, will be the weights or relative importances assigned to the characteristics.

This argument is based upon the fairly well-established fact that the psychological needs of most "normal" individuals are similar. Of course, the manner in which these needs may be filled (i.e., the value system) will vary considerably from individual to individual, and will be determined largely through enculturation. Similarly, the perceived relative importance of filling each of these needs or groups of needs will vary from individual to individual as well.

Perceived or conscious needs may also be culturally determined, or at least culturally reinforced too, but the primary determinant of an individual's hierarchy of needs will usually be his own sense of the degree to which his own needs have been satisfied. This hierarchy of needs is, in large part, synonymous with the individual's weighted list of QOL characteristics.

To the extent that particular socially, culturally, economically, or politically determined subgroups of a society experience relatively similar life environments, it is not unreasonable to assume that the individual members of such groups would have relatively similar sets of needs. From this supposition we may further expect that a set of QOL characteristic weights could be developed on a sample survey basis that would be fairly representative of all members of such a group, the extent of which might be defined by fairly simple sociometric data (income, education, race, family status, etc.). Admittedly, these would be crude measures but potentially useful for policy-evaluation purposes.

It is clear that a great deal of additional inquiry and data gathering will be necessary before we can substantiate any QOL concepts as imprecise as those put forward in this book. Inquiries similar to the first exercise with the Irvine group should be carried out with larger groups, representing a broad range of American social, economic, professional, and ethnic subsections. Suitable semantic equivalents for various characteristics across such groups must be developed to make such surveys possible. Only then can we begin to piece together the components of the overall set of needs and values that go into determining the QOL in America.

Similarly, an entirely new line of exploration will be needed to discover why surveys indicate there is an apparent decline in the QOL in the United States today. To study this, we would have to go beyond surveying and investigate actual decision situations, to look for the reasons why people opt for nonoptimal alternatives, and to determine the rates of occurrence and relative seriousness of such instances. This, of course, is a much more difficult pursuit than the simpler process of establishing the QOL characteristics and their relative weights. Further specific investigations on this point might be carried out in association with analyses of existing governmental programs.

The QOL characteristics, whatever they are eventually determined to be, should be potentially useful in the policy evaluation activities of public institutions. In fact, policy applications themselves should be extremely valuable in refining the characteristics, and in examining the question of barriers and restrictions to QOL optimization. For example, public surveys using the QOL characteristics could be used in evaluating alternative land uses, public housing units, neighborhood design, spatial planning, etc. The findings of such studies would at the same time be useful in telling us how in the past we may have acted to the detriment of the public's QOL.

To be totally useful to the policy maker, the QOL characteristics must be used in conjunction with an effective knowledge or understanding of the value systems of the various groups with which they are concerned. Inasmuch as these are sharply influenced by cultural factors and processes, they will be subject to a wide range of fluctuation. It will be particularly necessary for the public policy maker to keep in mind that there is a high probability that what his value system tells him would be an optimal mode of transportation or most attractive housing configuration may well be sharply suboptimal for a substantial portion of his constituency.

Summary

In this section, the QOL has been defined as the degree to which an individual or a society is able to satisfy the perceived psychophysiological needs. The level of the QOL is determined by barriers presented to the society and to its individual members in satisfying those needs. The medium of satisfaction is determined by the value system. This is a very neat, simple package in which to place the matter. Doubtless it is too neat and too simple but it is not an unreasonable point of departure.

A number of other theories regarding the determinants of the QOL have been put forward by others. Some deal with levels of aspiration. Some deal with positive and negative experiences. To our knowledge, none of the theories put forth to date conflict seriously with the approach put forth here, and, in fact, most are compatible. Reference may be made to the observation described earlier that American society as a whole is getting better in certain areas (e.g., knowledge and health) but getting worse in others (e.g., religious faith, happiness, moral conduct, inner peace). Limited data suggest that people in general place greater value on those things where we are slipping than they do on those in which we are excelling. Here, we are saying that people value highly those things that society does not provide them in adequate amounts to satisfy their needs. As their needs for education and health have been met, they have become increasingly aware of their needs for inner happiness and peace of mind. Hence, their relative QOL weights for health and education go down and those for happiness and inner peace go up.

In the end, we must bring the entire QOL investigation back to the policy makers, for it is they who are in a position to change the level of QOL in the United States. Similarly, it is they who must have a profound understanding of the components of the nation's QOL so they may be better guided in carrying out their responsibilities. In this context, "policy makers" does not refer merely to the decision makers of the public sector, but includes decision makers of the private sector as well, including the so-called taste setters and image makers who are instrumental in swaying the public with their sets of values and views of "things as they ought to be."

Finally, consideration of the QOL and its components should make us wary of the concept of political feasibility as a criterion for public policy makers. It should be clear that an action that is currently politically feasible may be distinctly suboptimal from the standpoint of the QOL of society as a whole, or at least a significant portion of it. This is particularly true given the rather cumbersome mechanisms for redress in our present-day institutions. Ultimately, a public institution making a great number of politically feasible decisions that are significantly suboptimal to its constituency's QOL may well lose its claim to legitimate authority.

Research Approaches

The earlier sections have described a general approach to the assessment of the QOL for an individual and some preliminary studies based on that approach. In general, the results of these studies have been favorable with respect to the fruitfulness of the approach. The material elicited by the exercises has been found to be compatible with the model, and as reported earlier in this chapter, the QOL assessment of a set of job opportunities produced preference rankings that are closely similar to independently obtained preference rankings. The aggregated general qualities appear to be interpretable by respondents at least for the university community we have been interacting with. However, some additional studies suggest they are interpretable by a wider population also.

These observations are supported by the results of a somewhat more extensive investigation undertaken to assess the effectiveness of Delphi procedures when applied to value judgments. These included four exercises, one with 20 alumni of the UCLA Executive Engineering Course, one with 12 wives of these alumni, one with 106 professionals at a conference on leisure, and one with 9 Venezuelan engineers in Caracas.[f] All groups rated the relative importance of the list of qualities in table 4-7. The lowest Spearman rank correlation among these set of four ratings was 0.79 between the Venezuelan engineers and the American engineers, all of the other rank correlations were 0.85 or higher.

This all adds up to a promising beginning. However, several crucial questions about the approach we have employed have received only partial answers. The most crucial, of course, is whether the structure of concepts that has been

[f]The data from this exercise was kindly furnished by Prof. Roy Lave of the Engineering School of Stanford University.

Table 4-7
Qualities Used in Four Delphi Studies of Quality of Life

1. Novelty (newness, surprise, variety)
2. Health (physical well-being, feeling good)
3. Dominance (superiority, power, control, aggression)
4. Self respect (self-confidence, self-understanding)
5. Challenge (stimulation, competition, ambition)
6. Freedom (individuality, spontaneity, unconstrained)
7. Comfort (economic well-being, good things, relaxation)
8. Affection (love, caring, relating, understanding)
9. Security (peace of mind, stability, lack of conflict)
10. Achievement (sense of accomplishment, meaningful activity)
11. Status (prestige, social recognition, positive feedback)
12. Involvement (participation, concern)

elicited has any useful tie to the effects that events actually have in shaping the sense of well-being of individuals. Our respondent groups think it has, and that is a nonnegligible item. Nevertheless, given the well-known looseness of fit between terms such as self awareness, status, novelty, etc., and actual experience, undoubtedly the reader (like the authors) would be happier if there were an independent way to show that the whole package is not hopelessly vague. This reasonable request is not at all the same as asking that the quality terms be completely precise and unambiguous. A vague term that allows some significant distinctions to be made is undoubtedly better than no term at all, providing it is used with due caution.

The issue of validity involves some important specific questions that are tractable with present techniques, as suggested below.

Research Questions

Identification and Completeness of Qualities. It is possible to multiply indefinitely (at least verbally) the list of properties of events that might be relevant to the QOL of an individual. Presumably the amount of overlap within this list is large. However, we hope the list can be compressed by finding a few general "dimensions" that sum up the contributions of the component items. This has appeared to be the case with lists generated by free responses in our exploratory exercises.

The issue of completeness arises in determining when to close off the list of dimensions. This is not simply a problem of eliciting a group of factors and eliminating those with low correlations with any of the specific items. In the factor analysis of many fields, it is assumed that a set of specific items exhaustively defines the area of interest. In the present case, we are concerned with the relationships between a set of factors and more global indexes, such as reported level of happiness, inclination to suicide, preference for various streams of events, and the like.

On the other hand, the situation is a good deal more complicated. An additional complication arises, at the level of our work, from the possibility that there may be quite different ways of slicing the world view, depending on various determiners, but in particular, sex. The evidence to date appears to indicate that male and female students have different QOL structures with which they rate life. The differences are not large, but are pervasive—i.e., they involve the way in which elementary descriptions form clusters on the basis of similarity ratings.

If the difference turns out to be primarily between men and women, the problem is probably not intractable. If the differences are sharply dependent on other determiners as well, then the approach may require major modifications, possibly along the lines of defining life styles dependent on various configurations of determiners.

Measurement (Scalability) of Qualities. The issue here is whether the qualities, once identified, can be furnished with practical independent scales. Strictly speaking, if a sufficiently comprehensive set of scalable descriptors can be found, then the cluster of items relevant to a given quality and the weights of those items (degree of relevance) furnish a scale. However, this is all very shaky, especially if it is necessary to assume, as in factor analysis, that there is a simple linear relationship between specific items and qualities. The model becomes much sharper and much more testable if it is possible to find separate scales for the qualities themselves.

This issue can be pursued apart from the identification issue, provided it is possible to persuade oneself that several qualities are sufficiently well defined to be worth working on. For example, a few qualities, such as novelty, freedom, feeling of accomplishment, have turned up in all the QOL exercises. One or more of these could be studied with regard to measurability.

Temporal Variation. This issue has several components, and part of the research problem is separating these components as well as evaluating their relevance to QOL. There are a number of basic considerations involved in making the separations. First, there are large variations in kinds of events, frequencies, affect level, and the like within a day, from day to day, and from week to week—not to mention longer time intervals. Apparently the contribution of this jiggle of events to perceived well-being smooths itself out to a surprising extent. Part of the smoothing is apparently accomplished by fairly radical discounting over time. A large variety of other smoothing functions could be considered—saturation effects, simple averaging, attending only to "highs," attending mainly to "lows," etc.

Also, much of the temporal variation appears to be a matter of mood—a rather mystical notion that connotes inexplicable changes of hedonic level from time to time, and is also used to describe equally inexplicable differences in hedonic level between individuals (one is moody, another happy, etc.).

In addition, surveys have indicated a rather high degree of mobility among the levels of reported happiness. However, the velocity of these changes—that is, the rapidity with which they occur—has not been pinned down. Is an individual likely to see himself as very happy one week, and not very happy a week or so later? Is most of the mobility accounted for by a subgroup of individuals with ups and downs or is it a reflection of major changes in the stream of events occurring to otherwise undifferentiated individuals?

One other topic in temporal variation, namely changes in comparison level, is discussed next.

Comparison Level. This issue involves the degree to which a notion of comparison level or level of aspiration must be introduced in order to account for the level of perceived well-being. The notion of aspiration level is a part of the body of explanatory concepts in social psychology—especially in the literary sociology of disadvantaged groups. There is a hint that some such notion could illuminate the apparent downward trend in perceived well-being that has been disclosed by public surveys.

Part of the issue is the formal structure the comparison level notion should take in the model. One simple form is the idea of a zero point for each of the dimensions, where the zero point is defined as the level at which negative feelings turn to positive—e.g., for novelty, the separation between mild boredom and mild interest. Furthermore, the zero points may not be fixed, but rather vary with the circumstances of an individual's life—and possibly with the general direction or slope of the event stream in QOL space.

This issue interacts with the issue of the functional form of the QOL "surfaces" in quality space, and the form of the global index. There is the question, for example, whether an aspiration or comparison level is attached to the global index, as well as to the individual qualities.

Global Function. Most component items in this issue have been mentioned above, but it is useful to review them under one heading. The stream of events introduces a number of complications into the analysis of QOL. The qualities are considered as characteristic of events; each event can be assigned a location in quality space. We can postulate tradeoff curves within the quality space, in which case a global index—call it Q—could be attached to each event. Then, overall well-being could be expressed as some function of the time pattern of Q.

The simplest such function would be an integral or average, with a time discount. More complicated functions might include a trend (upward or downward), the amount of variation, and so on.

The research problem posed by this complicated structure is rather severe. The most difficult aspect of the model is the use of events as basic elements. There does not appear to be any particular difficulty in identifying events, at least at the low level of sophistication contemplated for initial studies, and probably not too much difficulty in rating specific events in terms of qualities. The difficulty arises in attempting to sample the stream of events occurring within a postulated time horizon.

Research Approaches

The set of issues described above may at first reading appear to be a tangle of notions more difficult to sort than the maiden's heap of colored skeins in the German legend. However, we don't have to depend on the appearance of a magician to make progress. For one thing, no one's head will be chopped off if the job isn't completed in one night. For another, about all we want from the list of issues is a reasonable push in the direction of fruitful investigation. Several approaches are discussed below.

Delphi. A reasonable assumption is that most people have a fair amount of experience with and understanding of people. However, we would expect the experience of any given individual to be partial, and his understanding to be biased in many ways. Both of these difficulties can be compensated for to some extent by pooling the experience of a sizeable group of people, thereby extending the range of experience and letting biases cancel. Thus, one reasonable, if limited, approach is to assemble a group of knowledgeable individuals and pool their opinions systematically. This approach has been exploited in the studies described in previous sections.

A potential objection is that at the level of generality with which QOL is treated in the present discussion, individual opinions are value judgments rather than factual, and hence, are essentially subjective—i.e., neither right nor wrong. Our feeling is that there is no essential difference between these two realms of discourse, other than that value statements tend to be much vaguer and more loosely tied to reality than factual statements.

On the other hand, empirical research with value judgments as subject matter is feasible. Assuming that a significant body of value judgments can be expressed using at least an ordinal scale, much of the Delphi procedure is applicable. The rule "N heads are better than one"—which is the justification for using group judgments for factual estimation in areas of middling or low verifiability—is based on the simple observation that given any distribution of estimates of an ordered parameter by a group, the median of that set of judgments is at least as close to the true answer as those of one half of the group.[g] That is to say, if there is no way to distinguish among the answers, then there is at least a 50-50 chance that the group response (defined as the median) is better than any given individual answer. In actual situations with factual estimation, the median is generally better than the responses of more than half of the individuals.

In the case of value judgments, precisely the same justification for preferring a group response holds, providing a simple assumption is made. This assumption is that there is a correct answer to the value question. *Correct* does not necessarily mean objectively true, although that interpretation is not ruled out. All that is required is that there be an answer that, if everything were known, would be accepted as right. This assumption is very weak. Presumably, if it could not be made, there would be no point in the value judgment whatsoever. Note that the assumption does not mean that in a state of incomplete information there should be any particular degree of agreement within a group as to what the correct answer is.

Nevertheless, even in this weak form, the assumption has some content. In the first place, it requires that the judgment of an individual should have a certain stability; judgments cannot be capricious in the sense that (without further information) a given individual is as likely to say one thing as another. This property is very difficult to test because of memory. An individual who formulates and expresses a judgment is likely to remember and replicate the judgment some short time later.

The property can be tested in a weak fashion by asking a sizeable group the same question. We would expect a certain amount of variation of judgments, even among a group of highly similar individuals. If the distribution is flat or U-shaped, there is some basis for concluding that the group is not expressing a judgment.

A somewhat more tractable property is a special type of reliability—in this case, group reliability. Given two quite similar groups, we would expect that, on the average, the medians of individual responses would be similar. In addition, we would expect a kind of stability of group judgment, in the sense that changes attendant on iteration with feedback would, again on the average, converge in similar directions. This property can easily be tested by experiment.

In the exercises we have conducted so far, the three properties—intergroup reliability, reasonable distributions, and reasonable changes on interaction—have been exemplified. It would appear, then, that Delphi procedures result in group judgments that are more solid than just a summary of subjective attitudes.

---

[g]In order to say anything about "closer," it is, of course, necessary to have at least a ratio scale. It appears to be the case that reasonable approximations to ratio scales with "subjective" magnitudes of this sort involved in QOL estimation are relatively easy to obtain.

Cross-Sectional Survey. Despite some recent adverse publicity, national surveys dealing with perceived well-being have produced the most significant information concerning relevant aspects of QOL of any studies to date. There are reasonable grounds for believing that somewhat more carefully designed surveys might add a good deal better understanding of the subject. In particular, by focussing on quality and global index items, a fairly rich amount of data can be collected in a questionnaire of reasonable size. Assuming there are roughly ten major quality areas to be explored, and assuming something like 10 questions per area, a set of 100 questions would probably give as complete a coverage of qualities as could be absorbed at the present time. This leaves a liberal space for demographic information and policy-relevant questions.

It does not seem that a larger sample than the fairly common one of about 1500 would be needed. It would be extremely valuable to have a replication of the survey with the same sample after about a month's time to get some data concerning short-range time changes.

Some questions of detail remain. It seems likely that some sort of memory prod is desirable. Bradburn used the simple question "During the past week have you . . . ?"[15] Since this device appeared to be successful, a variation on it could be used to create recall. Then ratings of these events on other quality items could be obtained.

Scale Construction. The set of qualities for the QOL model offers a fairly rich area for the construction of scales. However, the techniques required are probably somewhat unorthodox as far as standard psychological scaling methods are concerned, and it is more than likely that each quality will require special handling. The problems arise mainly in attempting to develop intersubjective scales. The simplest form of ordered scale is a set of items that can be arranged in a series on the basis of some transitive and asymmetrical relation. A good example is Mohs' hardness scale, where the relation is "scratches"; any given solid can be assigned a place in the scale by determining the highest item in the standard list that it scratches. Applied to qualities, this would require a sequence of events ordered by the relation, more of quality x; for example, visiting in-laws involves less affection than going on a second honeymoon. A simple scale of this sort can be called intersubjective if the set of standard events has the same order for all individuals.

For individuals, it seems probable that rating a set of events with respect to a given quality would not be difficult, and a number of well-known procedures exist for determining whether a single scale is involved, and checking the consistency of a subject's judgments. However, for some of the qualities the ordering of a given set of events is likely to depend on the past experience of the individual. An event that is boring to one person may be interesting to another. The same issue arises in comparing events at different times during the life of the same individual. Not all the qualities appear to have this difficulty; the characteristic of freedom, or degree of control, seems to be more intersubjectively definable than novelty.

Novelty is certainly one of the more interesting of the qualities. There is a fair amount of evidence to suggest that if a situation is too novel it can be experienced in any of a number of ways as unpleasant. In addition, novelty appears to act like a scaling factor on other qualities; an unexpected unpleasant event appears even more unpleasant. There is probably no point in trying to disentangle this sort of intricacy without a fair amount of data to chew on.

It seems likely that progress in this area would be most rapid if two or three of the qualities were selected and worked on rather intensively, rather than trying to cover the entire set. This could be a little frustrating, however, since in our present state of ignorance there is probably a nontrivial amount of interaction among the qualities as they are presently perceived. However, much of this overlap would be identified in the attempt to produce well-defined scales.

It is too soon to ask whether anything stronger than ordinal scales can be constructed for items of the sort being considered. It appears clear that having even gross ordinal scales would constitute a big step ahead in any research program attempting to investigate tradeoffs or relative weights among the qualities.

Time Study. A most revealing investigation—if it could be carried out in full depth—would be an "event following" study, in which a group of individuals recorded and rated the major events that occurred to them in a quasi-continuous fashion over a period of several months. Obviously, certain concessions would have to be made to keep the recording from being intrusive on the events themselves.

Something like this has been tried; Wessman and Ricks conducted two studies involving Radcliffe women and Harvard men.[16] The students were asked to rate the day, before retiring, on twelve and sixteen items. The ratings involved items such as overall hedonic level, felt degree of freedom, sense of involvement, and so forth. A factor analysis of the ratings discovered only two factors: a general hedonic level and variability. One hypothesis to explain the collapse of the items would be that a day is sufficiently rich in different experiences so that an overall rating effectively "smears" the possible variety of qualities of individual events. Another possibility is that inclusion of the global index of hedonic level soaked up enough of the variation so that the remaining items added very little.

A rather modest study could be designed in which, say, some thirty or so subjects before retiring identified the four or five most salient events that had occurred during the day, and rated each in terms of overall hedonic level, the study continuing for say three months. It would be even better if they kept a running average each day of the global quality of the past week, but it is not clear whether the aftereffects of judgments made so close together would obscure the roles of individual events. It might be possible to include a control group to test this effect.

Although a modest study like this would not resolve several of the issues concerning time variations in QOL, it would furnish a highly valuable body of data. In particular, it should cast a great deal of light on the hypothesis that a large part of the variation in perceived well-being is directly traceable to fairly specific properties of the stream of events experienced by the individual.

Table 4-8 summarizes the preceding discussion of issues and research approaches.

Table 4-8
Approach Summary

Issue	Delphi	Survey	Scale Construction	Time Study
Identification and completeness of qualities	**	***	*	**
Global index	**	***	*	**
Time variation	*	*	**	***
Scalability	*	**	***	**
Comparison level	**	***	*	***
Relation to policy	*	**	— —	*

Note: The asterisk scale is to be interpreted as follows—
***Probably will establish significant relationships.
**Will furnish basically needed information.
*Will furnish useful data.

Notes

Notes

Chapter 1
Introduction

1. Albert H. Cantril and Charles W. Roll, Jr., *Hopes and Fears of the American People* (New York: Universe Books, 1971).

2. Norman Cliff, "Adverbs as Modifiers Multipliers" *Psychological Review* 66 (1959): 27-44.

3. Milton Rokeach and Seymour Parker, "Values as Social Indicators of Poverty and Race Relations in America," *The Annals of the American Academy of Political and Social Science* 388 (March 1970): 97-111.

Chapter 2
The Delphi Method: An Experimental Study of Group Opinion

1. See Norman R.F. Maier, "Assets and Liabilities in Group Problem Solving: The Need for an Integrative Function," *Psychological Review* 74, no. 4 (July 1967): 239-49; and H.H. Kelly and J.W. Thibaut, "Experimental Studies of Group Problem Solving and Process," in Gardner Lindzey (ed.), *Handbook of Social Psychology*, vol. 2, Addison-Wesley Publishing Company, Inc., Reading, Mass., 1954.

2. S.E. Asch, "Effects of Group Pressure Upon the Modification and Distortion of Judgments," in Eleanor E. Maccoby, et al., (eds.), *Readings in Social Psychology*, 3rd ed., Holt, Rinehart and Winston, London, 1958.

3. M. Girshick, A. Kaplan, and A. Skogstad, "The Prediction of Social and Technological Events," *Public Opinion Quarterly* (Spring 1950) pp. 93-110.

4. N. Dalkey, and O. Helmer, "An Experimental Application of the Delphi Method to the Use of Experts," *Management Science* 9, no. 3 (April 1963): 458-67.

5. T. Gordon, and O. Helmer, *Report on a Long-Range Forecasting Study*, The Rand Corporation, P-2982 (DDC No. AD607777), September 1964.

6. See Harper Q. North, "Technology, the Chicken—Corporate Goals, the Egg," in James R. Bright (ed.), *Technological Forecasting for Industry and Government*, Prentice-Hall, Inc., Englewood Cliffs, New Jersey, 1968; and John McHale, "Typological Survey of Futures Research in the U.S.," Center for Integrative Studies, State University of New York at Binghamton, June 1970.

7. Norman Dalkey and Bernice Brown, "Comparison of Group Judgment Techniques with Short-Range Predictions and Almanac Questions," The Rand Corporation, R-678-ARPA, May 1971.

8. R. Campbell, "A Methodological Study of the Utilization of Experts in Business Forecasting," unpublished Ph.D. dissertation, UCLA, 1966.

9. Dalkey and Brown, "Group Judgment Techniques."

10. Thomas Brown, "An Experiment in Probabilistic Forecasting," The Rand Corporation, R-944-ARPA (in preparation).

11. O. Helmer, *Systematic Use of Expert Opinions,* The Rand Corporation, P-3721 (DDC No. AD662320), November 1967.

Chapter 3
Experimental Assessment of Delphi Procedures with
Group Value Judgments

1. M. Rokeach, *Beliefs, Attitudes and Values,* Jossey-Bass, Inc., San Francisco, 1968, pp. 14-19.

2. Bertrand De Jouvenel, *The Art of Conjecture,* Basic Books, New York, 1967.

3. Maj. J. Martino, "The Paradox of Forecasting," *The Futurist,* February 1969, p. 20.

4. S.C. Johnson, "Hierarchical Clustering Schemes," *Psychometrika* 32, no. 3 (1967): 241-54.

5. S.S. Stevens, "Ratio Scales of Opinion," in D.K. Whitla (ed.), *Handbook of Measurement and Assessment in Behavioral Science,* Addison-Wesley, Reading, Massachusetts, 1968.

6. Hubert M. Blalock, *Social Statistics* (McGraw-Hill, New York, 1960) p. 170.

7. N.C. Dalkey, *The Delphi Method: An Experimental Study of Group Opinion* (The Rand Corporation, RM-5888PR, June 1969), p. 25.

8. Blalock, *Social Statistics,* p. 203.

9. B. Brown, S. Cochran, and N.C. Dalkey, *The Delphi Method, IV: Effect of Percentile Feedback and Feed-In of Relevant Facts,* The Rand Corporation, RM-6118-PR, March 1970.

10. Ibid.

11. Stevens, "Ratio Scales of Opinion," p. 197.

12. S.E. Asch, "Effects of Group Pressure Upon the Modification and Distortion of Judgments," in E.E. Maccoby, T.M. Newcomb, and E.L. Hartley (eds.), *Readings in Social Psychology,* Henry Holt, New York, 1958, pp. 174-83.

13. See his *Beliefs, Attitudes and Values* (note 1) and his article, coauthored with S. Parker, "Values as Social Indicators of Poverty and Race Relations in America," *The Annals of the American Academy of Political and Social Science* 388 (March 1970): 97-111.

Chapter 4
Measurement and Analysis of the Quality of Life

1. Raymond Bauer (ed.), *Social Indicators,* MIT Press, Cambridge, Massachusetts, 1966.

2. Bernard Berelson and Gary Steiner, *Human Behavior*, Harcourt and Brace, New York, 1964.

3. Robert S. Lynd, *Knowledge for What*, Princeton University Press, Princeton, New Jersey, 1939.

4. SRI Educational Research Center, *Informal Progress Report*, Stanford, California, August 1967.

5. *Goals for Americans*, Report of the President's Commission on National Goals, Prentice-Hall, Inc., Englewood Cliffs, New Jersey, 1960.

6. John O. Wilson, "Californians Lead the Best Life," *Los Angeles Times*, October 22, 1967, section 6, p. 7.

7. Gerald Gurin, Joseph Veroff, and Sheila Feld, *Americans View Their Mental Health*, Basic Books, Inc., New York, 1960.

8. Norman M. Bradburn, and David Caplowitz, *Reports on Happiness*, National Opinion Research Center, Aldine Publishing Company, Chicago, 1965.

9. Norman M. Bradburn, *The Structure of Psychological Well-Being*, ALDINE Publishing Co., Chicago, 1969.

10. Clark L. Hull, *A Behavior System*, Yale University Press, New Haven, Connecticut, 1952.

11. Judson S. Brown, "Gradients of Approach and Avoidance Responses and Their Relation to Levels of Motivation," *Journal of Comparative and Physiological Psychology* 41 (1948): 45-65.

12. George Kingsley Zipf, *Human Behavior and the Principle of Least Effort*, Addison-Wesley Publishing Company, Inc., Reading, Massachusetts, 1949.

13. Corlin O. Beum, and Everett G. Brundage, "A Method for Analyzing the Sociomatrix," *Sociometry*, 13, no. 2 (May 1950): 141-45.

14. Robert Durbin and Curt Tausky, "Career Anchorage: Managerial Mobility Motivation," *American Sociological Review*, 30, no. 5 (October 1965): 725-35.

15. Bradburn and Caplowitz, *Reports on Happiness*.

16. Alden E. Wessman and David F. Ricks, *Mood and Personality*, Holt, Rinehart and Winston, New York, 1966.

Appendixes

Appendix A

TO:

FROM:

SUBJECT: PRELIMINARY "QUALITY OF LIFE" QUESTIONNAIRE

This is a preliminary exercise for a study in the methodology of identifying and assessing the factors involved in Quality of Life. The follow-on will be relevant to investigations in the areas of transportation, civil order, housing and welfare, and other domestic problems.

There will be at least two rounds to the present exercise. The first will consist of filling out Questionnaire 1, below. For the second round, you will be furnished a summary of the results of the first round, and a request to take another "whack" at an amended questionnaire. Additional runs will depend on the apparent payoff after the second round.

In the questionnaire there is a list of factors culled from the literature. The list is a composite of what various social scientists have considered basic and important in determining the quality of life (QOL). The items are quite abstract and suffer from a great deal of vagueness. However, for this exercise we have not attempted a sharp definition, but have appended a list of cognate terms much in the spirit of a thesaurus. You are asked to assess each item on the list in terms of whether it is meaningful, important, and measurable. In addition, you are asked whether the list is complete, and if not to suggest further factors that are important and to give a rough estimate of the relative importance of the factors in your expanded list. (Incidentally, this is not a search for moral judgments, but an attempt to identify those aspects of the social "condition" that play a major role in human affairs whether they are desirable or not. We hope the factors are not products of a particular culture, but are ingredients in any.)

We are excluding from the list a large number of physical and biological considerations such as food, shelter and clothing, light, air, water, sex, stimulus,[a] and the like. The reason is not that these are not important—they obviously are—but for *most* of these items in the United States, basic levels are pretty well guaranteed (the only individuals who die of exposure, e.g., are those who are either adventuring or are the victims of rare accidents). Clearly these items enter in a more subtle fashion at other than subsistence levels. We hope the list of factors given includes these additional roles of the biological items—e.g., *health* will include proper diet, *novelty* will include the effect of heightened stimulation, etc.

---

[a] In the sense that a minimal stream of stimuli is essential for the proper functioning of the organism, as sensory deprivation experiments have demonstrated.

Proposed Factors Important in QOL

A. Health: well-being, longevity, survival.
B. Meaningful activity: employment, work, accomplishment.
C. Freedom: range of options, correspondence in time between interests and activities, leisure.
D. Security: stability, freedom from threat, peace of mind.
E. Novelty: variety, stimulation, excitement, richness of experience.
F. Status: influence, social standing, dominance, power, respect.
G. Sociality: affection, participation, mutuality, response, friendship, love, belonging.
H. Affluence: comfort, income, good things, wealth.
I. Aggression: self-assertion, anger, release of frustration, competition.

In addition to these factors, there is a global item that is usually given prominence: Balance—coherence, self-fulfillment, harmony.

In what follows we will assume (unless you object) that this element has to do with the relative weighting of the other sort of factors; i.e., it is a "second-level" consideration.

INSTRUCTIONS FOR QUESTIONNAIRE

In the accompanying questionnaire, *Meaningful?* involves two considerations: (a) Is the notion sufficiently clear to be useful? and (b) Is the item sufficiently distinct from the remaining items to be worth a separate listing? A "yes" answer means both, a "no" answer means one or the other doesn't hold.

The question *Measurable?* refers to whether the item is a quantity (or is related to a quantity) that admits of a scale. A "yes" answer is acceptable here, even if you do not have a suggested scale(s), if in your judgment, a scale is possible. *Suggested Scale(s)* refers to quantities that are clearly measurable and that, in your judgment, are sufficiently closely related to the factor in question to act either as direct measures or as useful stand-ins.

Relative Weight refers to the comparative importance of the factors for an "average American citizen"—not how important he perceives it to be, but how important it *actually* is, in your judgment. It is clear that at least some of the factors may have an overriding importance under some circumstances, e.g., the situation of complete deprivation. An individual close to death may consider health absolutely dominant; an individual in a situation that is utterly lacking in novelty may find the escape from boredom overpowering, etc. At some later iteration, we may want to explore these limits. For the time being, we are only exploring the trade-offs in the area of some "representative" situation. If the notion of an average or representative situation escapes you, use your own trade-offs. Answer this part of the questionnaire after you have added further factors that you think are important, or after you have decided that none need be added. The relative weight should be expressed by allocating some part of 100 to each factor. The relative weights should add up to 100. (The miscellaneous "other" factor is included to indicate that you feel something is missing but not identifiable.) You may want to give a zero weight to factors that you have assessed as meaningless.

The blanks K, L, M have been left for additional factors that you think important.

You need not sign the questionnaire. All we ask is that you remember your identification mark so that we can correlate answers on the two rounds.

Name or Identification

QOL: Questionnaire I

_____

Factor	Meaningful?	Measurable?	Suggested Scale(s)	Relative Weight
A. HEALTH				
B. ACTIVITY				
C. FREEDOM				
D. SECURITY				
E. NOVELTY				
F. STATUS				
G. SOCIALITY				
H. AFFLUENCE				
I. AGGRESSION				
J. OTHER				
K.				
L.				
M.				
X. BALANCE				

Appendix B

INSTRUCTION SHEETS FOR ALTERNATIVE ENVIRONMENTS (JOB OPPORTUNITIES) AND ALTERNATIVE MODES OF TRANSPORTATION QUESTIONNAIRES

Part I—Alternative Environments
Instructions

The following represents a series of job offers that you might hypothetically be offered upon completion of the UCI-Rand Educational Program. In considering these offers, disregard the fact that you may not feel technically qualified for any of them, but rather assume that each hiring organization is fully aware of your actual capabilities and potentials, and that each is satisfied with you.

We would like you to "rate" these offers, if at all possible, in terms of the characteristics or qualities identified in the Delphi Exercise on the Quality of Life. Of course, some of the characteristics may not apply, but many will.

For each alternative (1 through 8) fill out a qualities sheet in the following fashion:

a. If, in your judgment, a particular alternative environment would simply provide a satisfactory amount or degree of a particular quality, enter a "0" in the box on the right-hand side of the page.

b. If, in your judgment, a particular alternative environment would provide an attractively superior amount or degree of a particular quality, enter some positive number (e.g., +1, +5, +9, etc.) up to 10, to indicate the value *you* place upon that advantage in *that* environment.

c. If, in your judgment, a particular alternative environment would provide a detractive aspect with regard to a particular quality, enter some negative number (e.g., 1, 5, 9, etc.) down to −10 to indicate the value *you* place upon *that* disadvantage in that environment.

d. If you believe that a particular alternative environment would have no relation or bearing upon a particular quality, enter *"N."*

If there is some aspect of the environment you find particularly positive or negative that you do not feel is covered by the list of qualities, describe this aspect on the back of the appropriate quality sheet. Also, if there is (are) a particular component(s) of a quality (under "definition") that you feel has (have) a strong positive or negative relationship to a particular environment, underline or circle it (them).

After you have done this for each of the eight alternatives, rate the acceptability of each of the alternatives by placing a number in the upper right-hand corner of the quality sheet for each environment. Your first preference should be indicated by a number 1, second choice by a 2, etc. If one (or more) alternative(s) are unacceptable, indicate by placing "NA" rather than a number in the upper right-hand corner. For those that are not acceptable, indicate on the back of the form any changes in the environmental description that might make the job acceptable (e.g., an increase in salary from $X to $Y, or an increase in contract length from 2 years to 5, etc.). If no changes would make the job acceptable, indicate "NONE" underneath the "NA" on the front of the form.

ALTERNATIVE CAREER/LIVING ENVIRONMENT NO. 1

Your agency has been asked to "loan" you to AID for two years. Your salary would be $24,000 plus allowances (p.a.). You would be stationed in Saigon as a program analyst, supervising several staff members developing, evaluating, and reviewing development programs for a Vietnamese Province. You would work closely with provincial and national Vietnamese officials, and would travel to the province at least twice each month.

Your family would live in the American quarter in Bangkok, Thailand, where it would be given a large house and yard with several servants, and live in a community with about 2500 other Americans, plus a large number of families of other Western Diplomats. You would be able to fly to Bangkok at no cost to visit your family on weekends, as your work permitted, and you and your family would get a month's vacation back in the States after one year in Southeast Asia.

After this two-year tour of duty, you could return to your agency, or remain with the Foreign Aid Program, with no obligation to repay the expenses of the UCI-Rand Educational Program.

ALTERNATIVE CAREER/LIVING ENVIRONMENT NO. 2

You have been offered a job by an aircraft company in its Systems Division as a full working-level analyst on a large system analysis staff. Starting salary will be $22,500 p.a., with the strong probability of moving to senior grade analyst ($27,500 p.a.) after 3 years satisfactory performance. The company will also pay to move all your household goods to Los Angeles, and will pay up to $7500 toward the down payment on a new house here in Los Angeles. However, you will have to pay your agency your tuition at UCI and the living expenses reimbursed to you during your year at UCI. You will also have to sign a contract with the aircraft company for 3 years.

ALTERNATIVE CAREER/LIVING ENVIRONMENT NO. 3

You can return to your own agency as you currently anticipate. Please give the following data for the job you expect to occupy when you complete the UCI-Rand Educational Program.

AGENCY _____

CITY AND STATE _____

GRADE AND POSITION TITLE_____

BRIEF DESCRIPTION_____

ALTERNATIVE CAREER/LIVING ENVIRONMENT NO. 4

Dartmouth College, in Hanover, New Hampshire, has offered you the opportunity to set up and direct a Planning, Programming, Budgeting System (PPBS) Training Program at the college's Department of Public Administration. You will be able to draw upon other college departments for instructors, but you will generally prescribe course content and emphasis, and you will also teach one course in the program, covering material of your own choosing.

The salary will be $15,000 p.a. plus a large home on 5 acres of wooded land fronting on the Connecticut River. You will be able to walk to campus. A 3-year contract will be given to you, and you will be expected to work directly with the college for 2 years. During the third year, you will be on sabbatical, and you will receive your full salary, although you will be free to do whatever you like, e.g., travel, write, serve as a consultant to public or private organizations, or do nothing at all, etc. During the 3 years, your children will attend a special school run by the college for children of faculty members, tuition-free. Your agency has agreed to waive all obligations you have to them, provided you return to them following the 3 years at Dartmouth.

ALTERNATIVE CAREER/LIVING ENVIRONMENT NO. 5

The City of Wheeling, West Virginia, has offered you a newly created post as Assistant City Manager. You would be responsible for general coordination of all municipal government programs, as well as for the development and installation of a formal system analysis/PPBS operation throughout the city government. You would have a staff of five technicians and three clerks, whom you would personally hire. Your initial salary would be $19,000 p.a. You would be offered an initial contract of 2 years, renewable thereafter for periods of up to 3 years each. Once again, you would have to reimburse your agency for the cost of tuition and expenses for the year at Irvine.

ALTERNATIVE CAREER/LIVING ENVIRONMENT NO. 6

You have been offered a position as Special Assistant to the Mayor of Cleveland, Ohio. Duties would include review and evaluation of proposals and programs developed by various city agencies; the promotion of city-government-wide use of a system analysis/PPBS approach to planning and budgeting; plus special projects, as assigned by Mayor Stokes. The position would pay $21,000 p.a. and would be based upon a 1-year, renewable contract. Once again, you have to repay your agency for your tuition and living expenses while at UCI.

ALTERNATIVE CAREER/LIVING ENVIRONMENT NO. 7

You have been offered the newly created post of Director, Office of Planning and Program Coordination, Commission for the American Virgin Islands. This would be a Career Civil Service position, at the GS-14 level, with the probability of its being upgraded to a GS-15 within 4 or 5 years. You would work directly under the Commissioner of the Virgin Islands, and would be responsible for the formulation, installation, and continued operation of a PPB System for the Commission, which handles all governmental functions for the Islands, as well as the Virgin Islands Development Corporation. This would be a permanent assignment, inasmuch as your agency has agreed to waive your obligations to it for your UCI-Rand Educational Program costs.

The Virgin Islands Commission will pay for the cost of relocating you and your family (if any) to Charlotte Amalie, the capital city, in compensation for which you would have to agree to stay on with the Commission for at least 3 years.

ALTERNATIVE CAREER/LIVING ENVIRONMENT NO. 8

You have been offered a job by the new owners of the Instrument Company of Dayton, Ohio, a small space component manufacturing and research concern, doing business primarily with NASA and the Air Force through the testing facilities at the Wright-Patterson Air Force Base just outside of Dayton. The firm employs about 250 people, mostly scientists and technicians, and does several million dollars worth of business annually with the Federal Government in a variety of fields. The company was an early leader in the space technology field, but has lost ground in recent years. Profits have fallen off badly.

The new ownership is convinced that the company's problems are largely internal and mostly due to bad management. Throughout the organization, management, policymaking, and supervision are totally in the hands of scientists and technicians who have risen through the ranks, and who have no formal management training. Thus, the new owners are looking for a man to review and analyze all of the firm's operations, procedures, policy- and decision-making mechanisms. This man will be given a free hand to look into and question all aspects of the organization, and the ownership will back his decisions to the hilt. Inefficient operations will be reorganized and ineffective personnel dismissed. The new man can expect to meet strong resistance and animosity from current management.

The salary offered will be $20,000 p.a. for an initial 2-year contract period, plus a potentially valuable stock option. Subsequently, if you do a good job, you will receive a raise to $26,000 p.a. and a vice-presidency in the firm. The company will pay your relocation expenses to Dayton, Ohio, and will pay off your obligations to your agency.

CONCLUSION (Do this only after you have completed rating the eight alternatives)

a. If you have an opportunity to take a position of major responsibility in the city or county government in the community in which you grew up, would you accept it? (By a position of major responsibility, we mean something similar to those alternative environment choices shown for Cleveland, Ohio, 6, or Wheeling, West Virginia, 5.)

b. How would you rank such an opportunity among those offered you in the alternatives on the preceding pages (e.g., above 3, below 2, or No. 1, etc.)?

c. List the quality characteristics (if any) you think would be outstanding or very positive, in such a position.

d. List the quality characteristics (if any) you think would be wanting, or negative, in such a position.

e. Describe briefly (as were the alternatives) a career/living environment you think would be as close as possible to ideal and that would be reasonably commensurate with your skills and qualifications. (If one of the alternatives meets this description, merely cite it.)

f. Finally, the list of quality characteristics that we have used in this inquiry were generated by a Delphi exercise, where responses were sought largely upon the basis of how the respondents thought *most people* viewed life, events, and the quality or well-being of their lives. In this context, did you personally agree with the responses you put down, as being representative of most people, or do your views on what determines the quality of life differ significantly from those that you think most other people hold?

Differ _____   Same _____

Similarly, do you believe that your views, your value system, your own manner of evaluating your life is relatively unique, i.e., shared by only a few people, or is your value system more or less consistent with a large majority?

Relatively Unique _____   Consistent with the Majority_____

Part II—Alternative Modes of Transportation
Instructions

Currently, most of us travel to Rand twice a week, via privately owned vehicles, traveling about 110 miles round-trip. Generally, three cars make this trip on a reimbursed basis, with the average outlay of approximately $36.00 for each "Rand day." At the same time, we must spend about 2-1/4 to 2-3/4 hours on the freeway on the days when we go to Santa Monica.

No one is particularly happy with the current situation. Irvine would like to reduce its travel costs from the current $75.00 per week level. We would like to reduce the amount of time we spend upon the freeway. Rand officials would like to see us spend a full 8 hours at Rand on the days we go there. Thus, we search for alternatives. On the following pages are listed alternative modes of travel between the area of the Irvine campus and Santa Monica. Also attached are quality sheets containing the list of Characteristics of the Quality of Life that we just completed.[a] We would like you to rate these alternative modes against the quality characteristics, in the following fashion:

a. If, in your judgment, a particular mode of transportation simply provides a satisfactory level or degree of a particular characteristic, place a 0 in the box on the right-hand side of the paper.

b. If, in your judgment, a particular alternative mode would provide an especially attractive or superior quantity or degree of a particular characteristic, enter some positive number between 0 and 10 to indicate the value that *you* place upon that advantage for *that* particular mode.

---

[a]Included as table 4-2.

c. If, in your judgment, a particular alternative mode possesses some detractive aspect with regard to a particular characteristic or quality, enter some negative number between 0 and −10 to indicate the negative impact or value *you* place upon that disadvantage for *that* particular mode.

d. If you believe that a particular alternative mode has no relation to or bearing on a particular characteristic, enter an N.

If there is some aspect of a particular mode you find particularly positive or negative which you do not feel is covered by the list of qualities (other than the stated attributes of that mode—e.g., it is faster or cheaper), describe this aspect briefly on the back of the appropriate qualities sheet. Also, if there is some particular aspect of a Characteristic (under "Definition") that is strongly related (either positively or negatively) to a given mode, circle it on the appropriate quality sheet.

After you have completed this evaluation, please rate the alternative modes in order of preference, with 1 being a first choice, 2 being second, etc. Indicate ties with equal numbers. Place the rating number in the upper right-hand corner of the appropriate quality sheet. If any mode is unacceptable, place NA in the upper right-hand corner of the quality sheet for that mode.

ALTERNATIVE MODE NO. 1—CHARTERED LIMOUSINE

A chartered 14-passenger limousine could pick us up at Town Center at a specified time, drive us to Rand, then pick us up and return us to UCI in the evening. The cost to Irvine would be roughly equal to that of the current system, and it would save no time. However, it would free all participants from the chore of driving, and would free drivers' autos for use by their families. The potential accident rate would be slightly lower than that for the current method—approximately 3.5 deaths per 100,000 passenger-miles traveled.

ALTERNATIVE MODE NO. 2—HOVERCRAFT

A chartered Hovercraft could take us from the Pavilion at Newport Beach Harbor to the Main Pier at Santa Monica. The travel time would be about 35 minutes each way. The cost to Irvine, however, would be about $240 per day. The accident rate would be considerably lower than for the current mode, about 2 deaths per 100,000 passenger-miles.

ALTERNATIVE MODE NO. 3—AIRCRAFT

We could take a chartered twin-engine plane from Orange County Airport to Santa Monica Airport, and then taxi to Rand. The air fare would be $6 round

158

trip per person, plus 50¢ per capita taxi fare each way to and from Rand. The elapsed time of the trip, including the taxi ride, would be about 30 minutes each way. The accident rate for this mode (not including the 4- to 5-minute taxi ride) would be .1 death per 100,000 passenger miles. The total cost to Irvine for one day's operation would be $91.

ALTERNATIVE MODE NO. 4—CURRENT METHOD

You are already aware of the features of this mode. Its daily cost to Irvine is $36, and the accident rate is the highest of all alternatives—5.7 deaths per 100,000 passenger-miles traveled.

ALTERNATIVE MODE NO. 5—RAIL

We could catch a regularly scheduled train in downtown Santa Ana that would take us to downtown Los Angeles. We would catch the train at 8:30 A.M., and it would get us to the heart of Los Angeles by 9:30 A.M. We would then have a 15-minute taxi ride to Rand on the Santa Monica Freeway. In the evening, however, the train does not leave Los Angeles until 7:00 P.M., arriving in Santa Ana at 8:00 p.m. The delay between closing at Rand and leaving Los Angeles could be used for study, or we could eat. We could also eat on the train, which has both a regular dining car and a club car for sandwiches, etc. The primary advantage of the rail mode is the cost ($1.00 each for rail fare round trip per day, plus $1.30 daily per capita taxi fare), plus the low accident rate, about 1.1 deaths per 100,000 passenger miles. The total cost per day to Irvine would be approximately $29.

CONCLUSION (Proceed only after you have completed the evaluation of the transportation modes)

If Irvine were to offer to budget for a portion of a higher-cost mode, how much would you be willing to pay *out of your own pocket* for a more rapid mode?

A. For aircraft $ _____ per day at Rand.
B. For Hovercraft $ _____ per day at Rand.

DATA SHEET ON RESPONDENTS

1. Name _____ 2. Age _____
3. Agency _____
4. Position Title and Grade _____
5. Official Post of Duty _____
6. Where did you spend most of your childhood (elementary and high school years)? Give city and state. (If you moved frequently, give several cities you remember.)

_____
_____

7. Father's Occupation _____

Index

Anonymity:
  compared with face-to-face interaction, 23–25
  as feature of Delphi method, 20–21
Asch, S. E., 82n, 141 (2), 142 (12)
Attitude research, compared with Delphi method, 82–83

Bauer, Raymond, 86, 142 (1)
Berelson, Bernard, 86, 143 (2)
Beum, Corlin O., 143 (13)
Bias, as a constant in estimation experiments, 27, 51, 133
Blalock, Hubert M., 142 (6, 8)
Bradburn, Norman M., 86, 135, 143 (8, 9, 15)
Brown, Bernice, 141 (7), 142 (9; 9, 10)
Brown, Judson S., 143 (11)
Brown, Thomas, 38, 142 (10)
Brundage, Everett G., 143 (13)

Campbell, R., 24, 141 (8)
Cantril, Albert H., 1, 141 (1)
Caplowitz, David, 143 (8, 15)
Cliff, Norman, 7, 141 (2)
Changeability of response, hypotheses accounting for, 43–44
Cochran, S., 142 (9, 10)
College major, and accuracy in Delphi estimations, 43 (table), 44
Convergence of responses, in Delphi method, 35–36, 81
Cluster analysis, and quality-of-life components, 8–9
Committee decision-making. *See* Group judgment

Dalkey, N. C., 20, 141 (4, 7), 142 (9; 7, 9, 10)
Decision inputs, typology of, 13–15
Decision-making. *See* Group judgment
De Jouvenel, Bertrand, 55n, 142 (2)
Delphi method:
  accuracy of response, factors affecting
    college major, 43 (table), 44
    distributional estimates, 37–38
    feed-in of factual information, 48–54
    forms of feedback, 40–42
    group self-evaluation, 46–48
    intelligence, 42–43
    iteration and feedback, 29–37, 82–83
    learning hypothesis, tested, 38–40
    sex, 42–44
    simple iteration, 44–45

time allotted, 45–46 (fig.)
  anonymity as feature of, 20–21
  applicability to value judgments, assessed, 57–58, 80–83, 133–134
  changeability of response, 43–44, 81
  compared with attitude research, 82–83
  compared with other scaling techniques, 82, 137 (table)
  convergence of responses, 35–36, 81
  defining characteristics of, 2, 20–21
  desirable properties of, 21
  deviant distribution detection procedure, 75
  experiments in development of, 21–22
  fatigue effect, postulated, 49
  and "the right answer," 4, 8, 56–57, 134
  See also Estimation; Group judgment
Distributional estimates, and accuracy of response, 37–38
Diversity of viewpoints, reduction of, 8–9
Dominant individuals, in face-to-face discussion groups, 19
Durbin, Robert, 143 (14)

Effects of Education (EE) experiment:
  category composite labels, 61
  changeability of responses, 81
  convergence of responses, 81
  distribution of responses, 74–75, 81
  factors of EE, listed, 66 (table), 72 (table), 80 (table)
  hierarchical clustering procedure, 62–65
  method, 58–68
  rating scale (7-pt) procedure), 66
  results, 68–80
  split-100 (S-100) procedure, 66
  subjects, described, 59
  substantive content of results, discussed, 83
Environments, idealized, and QOL index, 111–118
Estimation:
  bias, as constant feature of, 27, 51, 133
  distributional *versus* point choice, 37–38
  as a learned skill, tested, 38–40
  nature of, 25–29
  See also Delphi method

Face-to-face interaction:
  compared with anonymous feedback, 23–25
  inherent problems of, 4–5, 19–20
Facts, feed-in of, and accuracy of Delphi estimations, 48–54

159

Feedback:
  as feature of Delphi method, 20, 21
  forms of, and response accuracy, 40–42
  and iteration, effects of, 29–37
  median *versus* true answer effects, 33–37
Feld, Sheila, 143 (7)
Figure-of-merit, defined, 6
Forecasting, growth of interest in, and
  Delphi, 20–21
Functional values, defined, 117–118
Futuribles, 55n

Girshick, M., 141 (3)
Gordon, 20
Group judgment:
  as basis of Delphi approach, 3–5, 10,
    20–21
  defining characteristics of, 57
  and diverse points of view, 7–9
  and face-to-face discussion, problems of,
    4–5, 19–20
  and group size, 18–19
  lowest common denominator fallacy, 5–6
  mean/median, differential usefulness of,
    16–17
  n-heads rule, 4, 15–20, 133–134
  performance evaluation of, 4–6, 10–11,
    22–25, 134
  reliability of, 17–19
  and population of potential respondents,
    18
  See also Delphi method; Values
Gurin, Gerald, 86, 143 (7)

Helmer, O., 20, 141 (4, 5), 142 (11)
Hull, Clark L., 90, 143 (10)

Individual optimization barriers, and QOL
  choices, 116–118, 121, 123, 125
Intelligence test scores, and Delphi accuracy,
  42–43
Iteration of experiments, effect of, 29–37

Johnson, S. C., 62, 142 (4)

Kaplan, A., 141 (3)
Kelly, H. H., 141 (1)
Knowledge, as type of decision input, 13–
  14 (fig.)
Kolmogorov-Smirnov (K-S) two-sample
  test, 75

Lave, Roy, 129n
Log-normal distribution of responses, 26, 74
Lowest common denominator fallacy, in
  group decision-making, 5–6
Lynd, Robert S., 86, 89, 143 (3)

Maier, Norman R. F., 141 (1)
Martino, J., 142 (3)
McHale, John, 141 (6)

N-heads rule, 4, 15–20, 133–134
Noise, semantic, in face-to-face discussion
  groups, 19–20
Normative values, defined, 117–118
North, Harper Q., 141 (6)
Numerical judgments, advantages of using,
  6–7

Opinion, as type of decision input, 13–15
Osgood, C. E., 7

Parker, Seymour, 141 (3)
President's Commission on National Goals
  (1960), 86, 143 (5)
Probability distributions for short-range
  forecasts, 38
Psychophysical scaling, compared with
  Delphi method, 82

Quality-of-life concept:
  attempts at clarification
    armchair lists approach, 86–91
    survey approach, 86, 91–92
  factors responsible for changing, 88
  future research approaches
    cross-sectional survey, 135
    Delphi, 133–134
    scale construction, 135–136
    time study, 136–137
  future research questions
    aspiration levels, 132
    global function, 132–133
    identification and completeness of
      qualities, 130–131
    scalability of qualities, 131
    temporal variation, 131–132
  general considerations, 9, 85–86, 89–91,
    126–128
  and public policy-makers, 128–129
  and time-distance variations, 90–91
  tradeoffs among components of, 9–11, 89
Quality of life, preliminary model for
  analysis of:
  aspiration level, 94
  behavioral implications of ideal model, 96
  "determiners," defined, 94–95
  discount rate, for past and future events,
    94
  expectation, as perceived future trajec-
    tories, 93–94
  "life," as sequence of events, 92
  payoff, in QOL units, 95–96
  scalable qualities of events, 93

tradeoff curves, 95
Quality-of-life experiment:
  category composite tables, 60
  changeability of responses, 81
  convergence of responses, 81
  distribution of responses, 74–75, 81
  factors of QOL, listed, 65 (table), 71
    (table)
  hierarchical clustering procedure, 62–65
  magnitude-estimation (M-E) procedure, 66
  method, 58–68
  results, 68–80
  split-100 (S-100) procedure, 66
  subjects, described, 59
  substantive content of results, discussed,
    83
Quality-of-life (QOL) index:
  and Delphi method, preliminary findings
    components, 99–102, 103–105, 130
    (table)
    method, 96–99, 147–149
    properties, 108–109
    subjects, described, 96
    time-dynamics, 102, 106–108
  experimental applications to decision-
    making
    barriers to individual optimization, 116–
      125 *passim*
    "desirability factor," formulation of,
      110–111
    ideal environments, ranking of, 111–118
    questionnaire, described, 110
    subjects, described, 109–110, 151–158
    tradeoff process, hypothesized, 114–125
      passim
    transport modes, ranking of, 118–125
  supporting research, 129–130
  variation across societal subgroupings,
    126–128

Ricks, David F., 143 (16)
Rokeach, Milton, 9, 83, 141 (3), 142 (1, 13)
Role values, defined, 117–118
Roll, Charles W., Jr., 1, 141 (1)

Scaling techniques, compared with Delphi
  method, 82, 137 (table)
Self-evaluation (group), and accuracy of
  Delphi estimations, 46–48
Sex:
  and accuracy in Delphi estimations, 42–44
  and differing QOL perceptions, 131
Skogstad, A., 141 (3)
Speculation, as type of decision input, 13–15
Split-half reliabilities, in estimating experi-
  ments, 28
Stanford Research Institute, 86, 143 (4)
Statistical definition of group response, as
  feature of Delphi method, 21
Steiner, Gary, 143 (2)
Stevens, S. S., 71, 82, 142 (5, 11)
Subjective magnitude scaling, compared
  with Delphi method, 82

Tausky, Curt, 143 (14)
Thibaut, J. W., 141 (1)
Time allotment, accuracy of Delphi esti-
  mations, 45–46 (fig.)
Time study, of QOL events, 136–137
Tradeoffs among QOL components, 9–11,
  114, 116, 121, 123–125
Transportation modes, and QOL index,
  118–125

Values:
  assessing the quality of, 3–4, 55–56
  and Delphi method, applicability of, 57–
    58, 80–83, 133–134
  need for clarification of, 1–2
  typology of, 117–118
  See also Group judgment
Veroff, Joseph, 143 (7)

Wessman, Alden E., 136, 143 (16)
Wilson, John O., 86, 143 (6)

Zipf, George Kingsley, 90, 143 (12)

About the Authors

Norman Dalkey is Senior Mathematician at The Rand Corporation, Santa Monica. He has done work in computer simulation, decision theory, and experimental evaluation of group judgment (Delphi). He has published numerous papers on these subjects and has chapters in various compendia on Long Range Forecasting, use of computers in the social sciences, systems research, and others. He is the author with B. Brown and S. Cochran of *Long Range Forecasting by the Delphi Method*, Dunod, France, 1972 (in French).

Daniel Rourke is Research Associate in the Behavioral Sciences Laboratory, Rockefeller University, New York. He received his Ph.D. in psychology from the University of California at Los Angeles in 1971.

David Snyder is Chief of Information Systems in the Internal Revenue Service, Washington, D.C. He is an Associate Editor of *The Bureaucrat*, and a private consultant on Urban Planning.

Ralph Lewis is Assistant Professor in the Department of Manpower and Management at California State University at Long Beach. He is also a Research Assistant in the Behavioral Sciences Department of the Graduate School of Management at the University of California at Los Angeles, and a consultant to The Rand Corporation.

Selected Rand Books

Bagdikian, Ben. *The Information Machines: Their Impact on Men and the Media*. New York: Harper and Row, 1971.

Bretz, Rudy. *A Taxonomy of Communication Media*. Englewood Cliffs, New Jersey: Educational Technology Publications, 1971.

Downs, Anthony. *Inside Bureaucracy*. Boston, Mass.: Little, Brown and Company, 1967.

Fisher, Gene H. *Cost Considerations in Systems Analysis*. New York: American Elsevier Publishing Company, 1971.

Goldhamer, Herbert, and Andrew W. Marshall. *Psychosis and Civilization*. Glencoe, Illinois: The Free Press, 1953.

Haggart, Sue A. (ed.) et al. *Program Budgeting for School District Planning*. Englewood Cliffs, New Jersey: Educational Technology Publications, 1972.

Harman, Alvin. *The International Computer Industry: Innovation and Comparative Advantage*. Cambridge, Mass.: Harvard University Press, 1971.

Hirshleifer, Jack, James C. DeHaven, and Jerome W. Milliman. *Water Supply: Economics, Technology, and Policy*. Chicago, Illinois: The University of Chicago Press, 1960.

Marschak, Thomas A., Thomas K. Glennan, Jr., and Robert Summers. *Strategy for R&D*. New York: Springer-Verlag New York Inc., 1967.

Meyer, John R., Martin Wohl, and John F. Kain. *The Urban Transportation Problem*. Cambridge, Mass.: Harvard University Press, 1965.

Nelson, Richard R., Merton J. Peck, and Edward D. Kalachek. *Technology, Economic Growth and Public Policy*. Washington, D.C.: The Brookings Institution, 1967.

Novick, David (ed.). *Program Budgeting: Program Analysis and the Federal Budget*. Cambridge, Mass.: Harvard University Press, 1965.

Pascal, Anthony. *Thinking About Cities: New Perspectives on Urban Problems*. Belmont, California: Dickenson Publishing Company, 1970.

Phillips, Almarin. *Technology and Market Structure: A Study of the Aircraft Industry*. Lexington, Mass.: D.C. Heath and Company, 1971.

Pincus, John A. *Economic Aid and International Cost Sharing*. Baltimore, Maryland: The Johns Hopkins Press, 1965.

Quade, Edward S. (ed.). *Analysis for Military Decisions*. Chicago, Illinois: Rand McNally & Company and Amsterdam, The Netherlands: North-Holland Publishing Company, 1964.

Quade, Edward S. and Wayne I. Boucher. *Systems Analysis and Policy Planning: Applications in Defense*. New York: American Elsevier Publishing Company, 1968.

Sharpe, William F. *The Economics of Computers*. New York: Columbia University Press, 1969.

The Rand Corporation. *A Million Random Digits with 100,000 Normal Deviates*. Glencoe, Illinois: The Free Press, 1955.

Williams, John D. *The Compleat Strategyst: Being a Primer on the Theory of Games of Strategy*. New York: McGraw-Hill Book Company, 1954.